AIR FRYER

OVEN

COOKBOOK

The Complete Guide to Gain Mastery Using Your Air Fryer Oven with Easy-To-Follow Instructions and Quick, Easy & Mouthwatering Recipes

AMBER MCBRIDE

TABLE OF CONTENTS

INTRODUCTION TO AIR FRYER COOKING

When I first heard about air fryers, I was skeptical. Another kitchen gadget, I thought, destined to gather dust in the back of my cupboard. How wrong I was! My air fryer journey began three years ago when my sister gifted me one for Christmas. Little did I know that this unassuming appliance would revolutionise my cooking and transform my kitchen habits.

At first, I stuck to the basics - chips, chicken wings, and the odd frozen snack. But as I grew more confident, I began to experiment. I discovered that my air fryer could roast a whole chicken to juicy perfection, bake a delightful chocolate cake, and even whip up a batch of crispy kale chips. It wasn't long before I was using my air fryer daily, marvelling at its versatility and convenience.

What struck me most was how the air fryer allowed me to create healthier versions of my favourite foods without sacrificing taste. Gone were the days of greasy takeaways and guilt-ridden indulgences. Instead, I was enjoying crispy, flavourful meals with a fraction of the oil.

As my expertise grew, so did my passion for sharing air fryer cooking with others. I started a blog, hosted air fryer dinner parties, and even taught a few classes at our local community centre. The joy on people's faces when they realised they could make restaurant-quality meals at home with minimal fuss was priceless.

This cookbook is the culmination of my air fryer journey. It's filled with the tips, tricks, and recipes I've perfected over the years, all designed to help you fall in love with air fryer cooking just as I have.

BENEFITS OF AIR FRYER COOKING

Air fryer cooking isn't just a trend; it's a revolution in home cooking that offers numerous benefits. Let me share with you why I believe every kitchen should have an air fryer:

1. Healthier Meals: Air fryers use hot air circulation to cook food, requiring little to no oil. This means you can enjoy your favourite fried foods with up to 80% less fat. It's a game-changer for those looking to reduce their calorie intake without sacrificing flavour.

2. Time-Saving: Air fryers cook food faster than conventional ovens. Most meals can be prepared in 15-20 minutes, perfect for busy weeknights or when you're in a hurry.

3. Energy Efficient: Air fryers use less energy than traditional ovens, which means lower electricity bills and a reduced carbon footprint.

4. Versatility: Don't let the name fool you - air fryers can do much more than just fry. They can roast, bake, grill, and even reheat leftovers. It's like having multiple appliances in one compact device.

5. Easy to Clean: Most air fryer baskets and trays are dishwasher safe, making cleanup a breeze. No more scrubbing greasy pots and pans!

6. Perfect for Small Spaces: Air fryers are compact, making them ideal for small kitchens, flats, or even caravans and motorhomes.

7. Consistent Results: The controlled cooking environment in an air fryer ensures consistent results every time. Say goodbye to unevenly cooked meals!

8. No Excess Oil: Unlike deep frying, there's no need to dispose of large amounts of used oil, making it a more environmentally friendly option.

9. Safe to Use: Air fryers are safer than deep fryers as there's no risk of hot oil splatter or fires caused by oil overheating.

10. Great for Picky Eaters: The crispy texture achieved by air frying can make vegetables and other healthy foods more appealing to fussy eaters.

HOW THIS COOKBOOK WILL TRANSFORM YOUR COOKING

This cookbook is more than just a collection of recipes; it's your comprehensive guide to mastering air fryer cooking. Whether you're a complete novice or an experienced cook looking to expand your air fryer repertoire, this book has something for everyone.

Here's what you can expect:

1. In-depth Understanding: We'll start by demystifying air fryer technology. You'll learn how these clever machines work and why they're so effective at creating crispy, delicious food with minimal oil.

2. Equipment Guide: I'll walk you through the different types of air fryers available, helping you choose the right one for your needs. You'll also learn about essential accessories that can enhance your air frying experience.

3. Getting Started: From unboxing to your first cook, I'll guide you through setting up your air fryer, including important safety precautions and maintenance tips to keep your appliance in top condition.

4. Mastering Techniques: You'll learn essential air frying techniques like preheating, shaking, and flipping. I'll also share my tips for achieving the perfect texture and doneness for different types of food.

5. Adapting Recipes: One of the most valuable skills you'll gain is learning how to adapt traditional recipes for the air fryer. You'll soon be air frying all your favourite dishes!

6. Meal Planning and Prep: I'll share strategies for incorporating your air fryer into your weekly meal planning, including batch cooking tips and ideas for quick, healthy meals.

7. Troubleshooting: Every cook encounters challenges. I'll address common air fryer issues and how to solve them, ensuring you achieve perfect results every time.

8. Diverse Recipes: From breakfast to dessert, healthy to indulgent, this cookbook covers it all. You'll find over 100 delicious, family-friendly recipes that showcase the versatility of your air fryer.

By the time you finish this cookbook, you'll have the confidence to create amazing meals in your air fryer. You'll be impressing family and friends with restaurant-quality dishes, all while saving time, energy, and calories.

SO, LET'S EMBARK ON THIS CULINARY ADVENTURE TOGETHER AND DISCOVER THE WONDERFUL WORLD OF AIR FRYER COOKING!

UNDERSTANDING YOUR AIR FRYER OVEN

TYPES OF AIR FRYER OVENS

When I first started exploring air fryers, I was surprised by the variety of options available. Understanding the different types can help you choose the best one for your needs. Here are the main types of air fryer ovens you'll encounter:

1. Basket-Style Air Fryers: These are the most common and what most people think of when they hear "air fryer". They're compact, usually egg-shaped or cylindrical, with a removable basket that holds the food. Perfect for smaller kitchens or for those who primarily cook for 1-2 people.

2. Oven-Style Air Fryers: These look like mini convection ovens and often come with multiple racks. They're larger than basket-style fryers and can cook more food at once. Ideal for families or if you want to cook entire meals in your air fryer.

3. Toaster Oven Air Fryers: These combine the functions of a toaster oven with an air fryer. They're versatile appliances that can toast, bake, and air fry. Great if you're short on counter space and want to replace multiple appliances with one.

4. Air Fryer Lid Attachments: These are lids that turn your existing pressure cooker or multi-cooker into an air fryer. They're a good option if you already own a compatible cooker and want to try air frying without investing in a separate appliance.

5. Built-In Air Fryers: Some high-end ovens now come with built-in air fryer functions. These are fantastic if you're remodelling your kitchen or replacing your oven, but they're the most expensive option.

Each type has its pros and cons, and the best choice depends on your cooking habits, kitchen space, and budget. In my experience, a good basket-style or oven-style air fryer is the most versatile option for most home cooks.

PARTS AND FUNCTIONS

Understanding the parts of your air fryer is crucial for using it effectively and safely. While designs may vary slightly between models, most air fryers have these basic components:

1. Basket or Tray: This is where you place your food. It's usually removable and has holes or a mesh design to allow hot air to circulate around the food.

2. Drip Tray: Located beneath the basket, this catches any oil or food debris that falls during cooking. It helps keep your air fryer clean and prevents smoking.

3. Heating Element: Usually located at the top of the air fryer, this is what heats the air.

4. Fan: This circulates the hot air around your food, ensuring even cooking and that crispy exterior.

5. Control Panel: This is where you set the temperature and cooking time. Some models have preset buttons for common foods.

6. Air Intake: Usually located at the top or back of the unit, this is where cool air enters the fryer.

7. Exhaust Vent: Hot air and steam escape through this vent, usually located at the back of the fryer.

8. Handle: Used to remove the basket or tray safely.

9. Safety Button: Many basket-style fryers have a button on the handle that must be pressed to remove the basket, preventing accidental drops.

10. Non-Stick Coating: Most baskets and trays have a non-stick coating for easy food release and cleaning.

UNDERSTANDING THESE PARTS WILL HELP YOU USE YOUR AIR FRYER MORE EFFECTIVELY AND TROUBLESHOOT ANY ISSUES THAT MAY ARISE.

HOW AIR FRYER TECHNOLOGY WORKS

The magic of air fryers lies in their ability to mimic deep-frying using hot air circulation. Here's a step-by-step breakdown of how this clever technology works:

1. Rapid Air Circulation: When you turn on your air fryer, the heating element begins to heat the air inside the cooking chamber. The powerful fan then circulates this hot air rapidly around the food.

2. Maillard Reaction: The hot air (usually between 150°C to 200°C) causes a reaction between amino acids and sugars in the food, known as the Maillard reaction. This is what gives food its brown colour and crispy texture.

3. Minimal Oil Use: Unlike deep frying, which submerges food in oil, air fryers require very little oil - usually just a light coating or spray. The hot air circulation cooks the food and creates a crispy exterior.

4. Even Cooking: The rapid air circulation ensures that heat reaches all sides of the food evenly. This is why it's important not to overcrowd the basket - you want the air to flow freely around each piece of food.

5. Moisture Removal: As the hot air circulates, it also removes moisture from the surface of the food. This is crucial for achieving that crispy texture we love in fried foods.

6. Temperature Control: The thermostat in your air fryer maintains a consistent temperature throughout the cooking process, ensuring your food is cooked evenly and to the desired doneness.

7. Timer Function: Most air fryers have a built-in timer that automatically shuts off the appliance when cooking is complete, preventing overcooking.

Understanding this process can help you get the best results from your air fryer. For instance, knowing that moisture removal is key to crispiness explains why patting food dry before air frying can lead to better results. Or why shaking the basket halfway through cooking ensures even browning.

THE BEAUTY OF AIR FRYER TECHNOLOGY IS THAT IT ALLOWS US TO ENJOY THE TASTE AND TEXTURE OF FRIED FOODS WITH A FRACTION OF THE OIL. IT'S A PERFECT EXAMPLE OF HOW KITCHEN TECHNOLOGY CAN MAKE OUR FAVOURITE FOODS HEALTHIER WITHOUT SACRIFICING FLAVOUR.

AIR FRYER OVEN VS TRADITIONAL COOKING METHODS

COMPARISON WITH DEEP FRYING, BAKING, AND GRILLING

As someone who loves to cook, I've experimented with various cooking methods over the years. When I first got my air fryer, I was curious to see how it would compare to more traditional methods like deep frying, baking, and grilling. Here's what I've discovered:

Air Fryer vs Deep Frying:

- Oil Usage: Air fryers use up to 80% less oil than deep fryers. You typically need just a tablespoon of oil or a light spray, compared to several cups for deep frying.
- Texture: While air fryers can achieve a crispy exterior, it's not quite identical to deep-fried food. However, the difference is minimal, and many people prefer the lighter texture of air-fried food.
- Safety: Air fryers are much safer to use, with no risk of hot oil splatter or fires from overheated oil.
- Cleanup: Air fryers are significantly easier to clean, with no large amounts of oil to dispose of.

Air Fryer vs Oven Baking:

- Cooking Time: Air fryers typically cook food 20-30% faster than conventional ovens due to their smaller size and efficient air circulation.
- Energy Efficiency: Air fryers use less energy than heating up a large oven, especially for small portions.
- Texture: Air fryers often produce crispier results than oven baking, especially for foods like chips or breaded items.
- Preheating: Air fryers preheat much quicker than ovens, usually in about 3-5 minutes.

Air Fryer vs Grilling:

- Weather Dependence: Unlike outdoor grilling, you can use an air fryer regardless of the weather.
- Smoke: Air fryers produce little to no smoke, making them suitable for indoor use without setting off smoke alarms.
- Flavour: While air fryers can't replicate the exact smoky flavour of grilling, they can achieve a similar charred exterior on foods.
- Versatility: Air fryers can handle a wider variety of foods than most grills, including baked goods and delicate items.

In my experience, the air fryer isn't a complete replacement for these methods, but it's an incredibly versatile tool that can replicate many of their best qualities while offering unique advantages.

HEALTH BENEFITS

One of the main reasons I fell in love with air fryer cooking is its potential health benefits. Here's how air frying can contribute to a healthier diet:

1. Reduced Oil Consumption: Air fryers typically use 70-80% less oil than traditional frying methods. This significant reduction in oil translates to fewer calories and less fat in your meals, which can aid in weight management and heart health.

2. Retention of Nutrients: The quick cooking time and lower temperatures used in air frying (compared to deep frying) can help preserve heat-sensitive nutrients in foods.

3. Reduced Acrylamide Formation: Acrylamide is a potentially harmful compound that forms in some foods during high-temperature cooking. Studies have shown that air frying reduces acrylamide formation by up to 90% compared to deep frying.

4. Encourages Vegetable Consumption: The crispy texture achieved by air frying can make vegetables more appealing, potentially increasing your intake of these nutrient-rich foods.

5. Less Trans Fat: By reducing the need for deep-fried foods, which are often high in trans fats, air frying can help lower your intake of these harmful fats linked to heart disease.

6. Portion Control: Many air fryers have a limited capacity, which can naturally encourage smaller portion sizes.

7. Reduced Risk of Consuming Oxidized Oil: Deep frying oil that's reused multiple times can become oxidized, potentially leading to the formation of harmful compounds. With air frying, this risk is eliminated.

While it's important to note that simply using an air fryer doesn't automatically make all foods healthy, it does provide a way to enjoy traditionally fried foods in a healthier manner. As with any cooking method, the overall healthiness of your meals will depend on the ingredients you use and your overall diet.

ENERGY EFFICIENCY

In today's world, where we're all trying to be more environmentally conscious and reduce our energy bills, the energy efficiency of our kitchen appliances matters. This is another area where air fryers shine. Here's why:

1. Faster Cooking Times: Air fryers cook food faster than conventional ovens, which means they use energy for a shorter period. For example, a batch of chips that might take 25-30 minutes in a regular oven could be done in 15-20 minutes in an air fryer.

2. No Preheating: While some recipes might call for preheating your air fryer, it's often unnecessary. Even when preheating is needed, it takes just 2-3 minutes compared to the 10-15 minutes a conventional oven might require.

3. Smaller Size: Air fryers have a much smaller cooking chamber than full-sized ovens. This means less energy is required to heat the cooking space.

4. Efficient Heat Distribution: The powerful fan in an air fryer circulates hot air efficiently, ensuring even cooking without wasting energy.

5. Lower Cooking Temperatures: Often, you can set your air fryer to a lower temperature than you would a conventional oven and still achieve the same results, further reducing energy consumption.

6. Multi-Functionality: Many air fryers can replace several appliances (like toaster ovens, deep fryers, and in some cases, microwaves), potentially reducing overall kitchen energy use.

7. Reduced Air Conditioning Costs: Using an air fryer generates less heat in your kitchen compared to using a full-sized oven, which could lead to savings on cooling costs in warmer months.

To give you a concrete example, let's compare cooking a chicken breast in an air fryer versus a conventional oven:

Conventional Oven: Preheating (10 mins) + Cooking (25 mins) = 35 mins total at about 2100 watts

Air Fryer: No preheating + Cooking (15 mins) = 15 mins total at about 1500 watts

In this example, the air fryer uses significantly less energy due to both the shorter cooking time and lower wattage. Over time, these energy savings can add up, potentially reducing your electricity bill and your carbon footprint.

It's worth noting that the exact energy savings will vary depending on your specific appliances, cooking habits, and local energy costs. However, in general, air fryers are a more energy-efficient option for many cooking tasks, especially when cooking smaller portions or items that benefit from crispy textures.

In my household, I've noticed a decrease in our energy bills since we started using the air fryer more frequently, particularly for meals that I would have previously used the oven for. It's just another reason why I believe air fryers are a fantastic addition to any kitchen.

GETTING STARTED

UNBOXING AND SETTING UP YOUR AIR FRYER OVEN

I remember the excitement of unboxing my first air fryer. It felt like Christmas morning! Here's a step-by-step guide to help you set up your new air fryer safely and correctly:

1. Unboxing:

   - Carefully remove the air fryer from its packaging.

   - Check that all components are present (refer to your user manual for a list of included parts).

   - Remove any protective materials, such as plastic wrapping or cardboard inserts.

2. Cleaning:

   - Before first use, wash the removable parts (basket, tray, etc.) with warm, soapy water.

   - Dry all parts thoroughly.

   - Wipe the interior and exterior of the main unit with a damp cloth (don't submerge the main unit in water!).

3. Placement:

   - Choose a flat, heat-resistant surface with good ventilation.

   - Ensure there's at least 10cm of free space on all sides of the air fryer.

   - Keep it away from walls, cupboards, and other appliances to prevent heat damage.

4. Assembly:

   - If your model has multiple parts (like a separate basket and drip tray), assemble them according to the manual.

   - Make sure all parts are securely in place.

5. Initial Test Run:

   - Plug in your air fryer.

   - Run it empty at 200°C for about 10 minutes. This helps remove any manufacturing residues and ensures everything is working correctly.

   - You might notice a slight odour during this first run - that's normal and will dissipate.

6. Familiarize Yourself with Controls:

   - Practice setting the temperature and timer.

   - If your model has preset functions, learn what each one does.

REMEMBER, EACH AIR FRYER MODEL MIGHT HAVE SLIGHTLY DIFFERENT SETUP INSTRUCTIONS, SO ALWAYS REFER TO YOUR SPECIFIC USER MANUAL FOR THE MOST ACCURATE GUIDANCE.

SAFETY PRECAUTIONS

Safety should always be a top priority in the kitchen. Here are some important safety precautions to keep in mind when using your air fryer:

1. Placement: Always use your air fryer on a flat, heat-resistant surface. Keep it away from walls, curtains, or any flammable materials.

2. Ventilation: Ensure proper air circulation around the appliance. Don't block the air intake or exhaust vents.

3. Electrical Safety:

   - Never immerse the main unit, cord, or plug in water.

   - Don't use the air fryer if the cord or plug is damaged.

   - Always plug into a grounded outlet.

   - Unplug the air fryer when not in use.

4. Hot Surfaces: The exterior of the air fryer can get hot during use. Use oven mitts or tongs when handling the basket or any hot parts.

5. Steam: Be cautious when opening the air fryer during or after cooking. Hot steam can escape and cause burns.

6. Overfilling: Don't overfill the basket. This can lead to uneven cooking and potentially cause food to touch the heating element.

7. Oil Use: While air fryers use less oil, be careful not to use too much. Excess oil can drip onto the heating element and cause smoking.

8. Food Safety: Always ensure meats are cooked to safe internal temperatures. Use a food thermometer if you're unsure.

9. Cleaning: Wait for the air fryer to cool completely before cleaning. Never use metal utensils or abrasive materials to clean the non-stick surfaces.

10. Children: Keep children away from the air fryer during use and for some time after, as it remains hot.

11. Fire Safety: Never leave the air fryer unattended while in use. If you see smoke, unplug the air fryer immediately.

12. Proper Use: Only use your air fryer for its intended purpose. Don't try to deep fry or fill it with oil like a traditional fryer.

BY FOLLOWING THESE SAFETY PRECAUTIONS, YOU'LL ENSURE A SAFE AND ENJOYABLE AIR FRYING EXPERIENCE. REMEMBER, SAFETY FIRST, DELICIOUS FOOD SECOND!

CLEANING AND MAINTENANCE

Proper cleaning and maintenance of your air fryer not only ensures hygiene but also extends the lifespan of your appliance. Here's my routine for keeping my air fryer in top condition:

After Each Use:

1. Unplug the air fryer and let it cool completely.

2. Remove the basket and/or trays.

3. Wash removable parts with warm, soapy water. Most are dishwasher safe, but check your manual to be sure.

4. For stubborn food residues, soak the parts in hot water for about 10 minutes before cleaning.

5. Wipe the interior with a damp cloth or sponge. Be gentle with the heating element.

6. Clean the exterior with a damp cloth.

7. Dry all parts thoroughly before reassembling.

Deep Clean (Monthly or as needed):

1. Create a paste with baking soda and water.

2. Apply this paste to any areas with built-up grease or food residue.

3. Let it sit for about 15 minutes, then wipe clean with a damp cloth.

4. For the heating element, use a soft brush to gently remove any food particles.

Maintenance Tips:

1. Always use non-abrasive tools to clean your air fryer to protect the non-stick coating.

2. Avoid using metal utensils in your air fryer as they can scratch the basket.

3. If you notice any peeling of the non-stick coating, stop using the air fryer and contact the manufacturer.

4. Regularly check the cord and plug for any signs of wear or damage.

5. If your air fryer has a removable door, clean both sides of the glass regularly to maintain visibility.

Odour Control:

If you notice lingering food smells:

1. Cut a lemon in half and place it in the basket.

2. Run the air fryer at 200°C for about 3 minutes.

3. The lemon will help neutralize odours.

Storage:

1. Ensure all parts are completely dry before storing.

2. Store in a clean, dry place.

3. If possible, leave the basket slightly open to prevent moisture buildup.

REMEMBER, A CLEAN AIR FRYER IS A HAPPY AIR FRYER! REGULAR CLEANING AND MAINTENANCE WILL ENSURE YOUR APPLIANCE CONTINUES TO PRODUCE DELICIOUS, CRISPY FOOD FOR YEARS TO COME.

ESSENTIAL TECHNIQUES
Preheating

When I first started using my air fryer, I was unsure about preheating. Do I really need to do it? How long should I preheat for? Through trial and error, I've learned that preheating can make a significant difference in your cooking results, especially for certain types of food. Here's what you need to know:

Why Preheat?

- Preheating ensures that your food starts cooking immediately when you put it in the air fryer.

- It helps achieve a crispier exterior on foods like chips, chicken wings, or breaded items.

- Preheating can lead to more even cooking, especially for thinner or pre-cooked foods.

When to Preheat:

- For foods that benefit from a crispy exterior (chips, breaded items, frozen foods)

- When cooking thinner cuts of meat or fish

- When reheating leftovers

When You Can Skip Preheating:

- For thicker cuts of meat that need to cook more slowly

- When baking cakes or bread

- For more delicate foods that might dry out with intense initial heat

How to Preheat:

1. Set your air fryer to the desired cooking temperature.

2. Run it empty for 2-5 minutes (refer to your manual for specific recommendations).

3. Once preheated, carefully add your food to the basket and begin cooking.

Preheating Tips:

- Most air fryers preheat much faster than conventional ovens, usually in 2-3 minutes.

- If your air fryer doesn't have a preheat setting, simply set the temperature and let it run empty for a few minutes.

- Be cautious when adding food to a preheated air fryer - the basket will be hot!

Remember, while preheating can improve results for many recipes, it's not always necessary. As you become more familiar with your air fryer and different recipes, you'll develop a sense of when preheating is beneficial and when you can skip it.

Shaking and Flipping

One of the key techniques for achieving evenly cooked, crispy food in an air fryer is shaking the basket or flipping the food during cooking. Here's why it's important and how to do it effectively:

Why Shake or Flip?

- Ensures even cooking and browning on all sides

- Prevents food from sticking together

- Helps achieve a uniformly crispy texture

When to Shake or Flip:

- For smaller items like chips, vegetables, or nuggets: Shake the basket

- For larger items like chicken breasts or fish fillets: Flip with tongs

How Often?

- For most recipes, shaking or flipping once halfway through cooking is sufficient

- For longer cooking times or when you want extra crispiness, you might shake or flip 2-3 times during cooking

Technique:

1. Carefully remove the basket or open the air fryer door

2. If shaking: Give the basket a good shake to redistribute the food

3. If flipping: Use tongs to carefully turn over larger items

4. Return the basket or close the door quickly to maintain temperature

Tips:

- Use heat-resistant gloves or oven mitts when handling the hot basket

- Some air fryers will automatically pause when you remove the basket; others will continue running, so be quick

- For delicate foods, use a spatula to gently turn them instead of shaking

- If your air fryer has multiple trays, rotate their positions for even cooking

Foods That Benefit Most from Shaking/Flipping:

- Chips and other potato dishes

- Vegetables like brussels sprouts or broccoli florets

- Chicken wings or nuggets

- Breaded items like fish fingers or mozzarella sticks

Remember, not all foods need shaking or flipping. Dense items like a whole chicken or a meatloaf can usually cook without interference. Always refer to your recipe or use your judgement based on how the food looks partway through cooking.

Using Oil Sprays

One of the great benefits of air frying is the ability to achieve crispy, "fried" results with minimal oil. However, using a small amount of oil can enhance flavour, texture, and browning. Here's my guide to using oil sprays effectively in your air fryer:

Why Use Oil?

- Enhances crispiness and browning

- Helps seasonings stick to food

- Prevents food from drying out

- Adds flavour

How Much Oil?

- Generally, you need only 1-2 teaspoons of oil for most recipes

- For a 1 kg batch of chips, I typically use about 1 tablespoon of oil

Types of Oil to Use:

- Oils with high smoke points work best (e.g., avocado, grapeseed, or light olive oil)

- Avoid olive oil with low smoke points as it can create smoke and off-flavours at high temperatures

Application Methods:

1. Oil Sprayer:

  - My preferred method

  - Allows for even, light coverage

  - Refillable options are more eco-friendly than aerosol cans

2. Brush:

  - Good for larger, flat items

  - Allows for precise application

3. Toss in a Bowl:

  - Ideal for small, numerous items like vegetables or chips

  - Mix food with oil in a bowl before adding to the air fryer

Tips for Using Oil Sprays:

- Always spray the food, not the basket (spraying the basket can damage the non-stick coating over time)

- For extra crispiness, lightly spray food again halfway through cooking when you shake or flip

- If using aerosol sprays, check that they don't contain propellants or additives that could damage your air fryer

- For foods prone to drying out (like chicken breasts), a light oil spray can help retain moisture

Oil-Free Options:

- Use egg wash or milk for breading instead of oil

- Some foods (like frozen chips) often don't need added oil

Remember, while a little oil can enhance your air fryer results, it's not always necessary. Experiment with different amounts to find what works best for your recipes and taste preferences. The goal is to use just enough oil to get the desired results while still maintaining the health benefits of air frying.

ADJUSTING TIME AND TEMPERATURE

Mastering the art of adjusting time and temperature is key to getting the best results from your air fryer. Here's my guide to help you navigate these crucial settings:

Understanding Your Air Fryer:

- Most air fryers can be set between 150°C and 200°C

- Cooking times typically range from 5 to 25 minutes

- Remember, air fryers cook faster than conventional ovens

General Guidelines:

- Higher temperatures (190-200°C): Best for foods that benefit from quick, crispy cooking (chips, chicken wings)

- Medium temperatures (170-180°C): Ideal for most meats, vegetables, and baked goods

- Lower temperatures (150-160°C): Good for more delicate foods or when you want to cook something more slowly

Adjusting for Different Foods:

1. Frozen Foods:

  - Usually require higher temperatures (190-200°C)

  - May need slightly longer cooking times than fresh foods

2. Meats:

  - Thinner cuts: Higher temp, shorter time

- Thicker cuts: Lower temp, longer time

- Always check internal temperature for food safety

3. Vegetables:

  - Hard vegetables (potatoes, carrots): 180-190°C, 15-20 minutes

  - Softer vegetables (zucchini, peppers): 170-180°C, 10-15 minutes

4. Baked Goods:

  - Generally require lower temperatures (160-170°C) and careful timing

Factors That May Require Adjustments:

1. Quantity of Food:

  - More food generally requires longer cooking time

  - Avoid overcrowding; cook in batches if necessary

2. Size and Thickness:

  - Larger, thicker items need lower temps and longer times

  - Cut foods into uniform sizes for even cooking

3. Personal Preference:

  - For crispier results: Increase temperature slightly or extend cooking time

  - For more tender results: Decrease temperature and possibly increase time

4. Your Specific Air Fryer:

  - Air fryers can vary, so you may need to adjust based on your model

  - Keep notes on what works best for your favourite recipes

Tips for Success:

- Start checking food a few minutes before the recipe's suggested time

- For new recipes, start with a lower temperature - you can always cook longer, but you can't undo overcooking

- Use the pause function to check food without losing too much heat

- Invest in a good kitchen thermometer for checking meat temperatures

REMEMBER, THESE ARE GENERAL GUIDELINES. THE BEST WAY TO MASTER YOUR AIR FRYER IS THROUGH PRACTICE AND OBSERVATION. DON'T BE AFRAID TO EXPERIMENT AND ADJUST BASED ON YOUR PREFERENCES AND THE RESULTS YOU'RE SEEING. HAPPY AIR FRYING!

AIR FRYER OVEN ACCESSORIES

MUST-HAVE TOOLS

When I first got my air fryer, I thought the appliance itself was all I needed. But over time, I've discovered that a few key accessories can really enhance the air frying experience. Here are the must-have tools I recommend:

1. Oil Mister/Spray Bottle:

   - Allows for even, light oil application

   - Refillable options are more eco-friendly than aerosol cans

   - Look for ones specifically designed for oil to prevent clogging

2. Tongs:

   - Essential for flipping foods and removing them safely

   - Silicone-tipped tongs are ideal to prevent scratching the non-stick coating

3. Silicone Brush:

   - Great for applying marinades or egg wash

   - Heat-resistant and won't scratch the basket

4. Instant-Read Thermometer:

   - Ensures meats are cooked to safe temperatures

   - Helps prevent overcooking

5. Silicone Pot Holders or Oven Mitts:

   - Essential for safely handling the hot basket or trays

   - Silicone offers better grip and heat resistance than fabric mitts

6. Parchment Paper Liners:

   - Makes cleanup easier, especially for messy or sticky foods

   - Ensure you get ones specifically designed for air fryers with holes for air circulation

7. Cooking Rack:

   - Allows you to cook on multiple levels, increasing capacity

   - Great for foods that need air circulation underneath (like bacon)

8. Baking Pan:

   - Useful for foods that might drip or for baking cakes and breads

   - Make sure to get one that fits your air fryer model

9. Silicone Trivet:

   - Protects your countertop when you need to set down the hot basket

10. Cleaning Brush:

   - A soft-bristled brush helps clean hard-to-reach areas without damaging the non-stick coating

11. Food Scissors:

   - Useful for cutting foods directly in the basket, like pizza or herbs

12. Silicone Spatula:

   - Great for removing delicate foods from the basket without scratching

These tools will help you get the most out of your air fryer, making cooking easier and more efficient. Remember, you don't need to buy everything at once - start with the basics and add more as you expand your air frying repertoire.

OPTIONAL GADGETS TO ENHANCE YOUR COOKING

While the must-have tools cover the basics, there are some optional gadgets that can take your air frying to the next level. Here are some I've found particularly useful:

1. Air Fryer Divider:

   - Allows you to cook different foods simultaneously without mixing flavours

   - Great for picky eaters or when preparing multiple components of a meal

2. Grill Pan:

   - Creates attractive grill marks on meats and vegetables

   - Helps drain excess fat away from food

3. Pizza Pan:

   - Perfect for making personal-sized pizzas or reheating slices

   - Often comes with a perforated design for optimal air circulation

4. Silicone Cupcake Liners:

   - Great for making individual portions of egg bites, mini quiches, or muffins

   - Reusable and easy to clean

5. Egg Bite Mold:

   - Ideal for making perfect egg bites or mini frittatas

   - Usually made of silicone for easy food release

6. Mesh Crisper Tray:

   - Provides extra elevation for even crispier results

   - Particularly good for items like chips or chicken wings

7. Bread Pan:

   - For baking small loaves of bread or meatloaf in your air fryer

   - Look for one that fits comfortably in your air fryer basket

8. Kebab Set:

   - Includes skewers and a rack for making kebabs in your air fryer

   - Allows for even cooking on all sides

9. Silicone Baking Cups:

   - Great for making individual desserts or portioning out snacks

   - Heat-resistant and reusable

10. Air Fryer Liners:

    - Disposable liners that make cleanup even easier

    - Ensure they're made specifically for air fryers with proper ventilation

11. Digital Kitchen Scale:

    - Helps with portioning and following recipes accurately

    - Particularly useful for baking in the air fryer

12. Marinade Injector:

    - For infusing meats with flavour before air frying

    - Can help keep larger cuts of meat moist during cooking

Remember, while these gadgets can be fun and potentially useful, they're not essential for great air fryer cooking. It's best to start with the basics and gradually add items as you discover your air frying preferences and expand your recipe repertoire. Always ensure any accessory you buy is compatible with your specific air fryer model and size.

MEAL PLANNING AND PREP

WEEKLY MEAL PLANNING STRATEGIES

Incorporating your air fryer into your weekly meal planning can save you time, reduce stress, and help you eat healthier. Here are some strategies I've found effective:

1. Theme Nights:

   - Assign themes to different nights of the week (e.g., Meatless Monday, Taco Tuesday, Fry-day)

   - Use your air fryer to create dishes that fit these themes

2. Batch Cooking:

   - Cook larger portions of staples like chicken breasts or roasted vegetables

   - Use these in various dishes throughout the week

3. Prep Ahead:

   - Cut vegetables, marinate meats, or prepare breading mixes in advance

   - Store prepped ingredients in the fridge for quick cooking during the week

4. Leftovers Plan:

   - Plan to use leftovers in new ways (e.g., leftover roast chicken in a salad or wrap)

   - The air fryer is great for crisping up leftovers

5. Balance Your Meals:

   - Aim for a mix of proteins, vegetables, and carbohydrates in your weekly plan

   - Use the air fryer to prepare a variety of foods for balanced meals

6. Consider Your Schedule:

   - Plan quicker air fryer meals for busy nights

   - Save more involved recipes for when you have more time

7. Create a Rotating Menu:

   - Develop a 2-3 week rotating menu of air fryer favourites

   - This reduces decision fatigue while ensuring variety

8. Use a Meal Planning App or Template:

   - Many apps allow you to save recipes and generate shopping lists

   - Or create a simple spreadsheet or use a physical planner

9. Plan for Flexibility:

   - Have some quick, pantry-based air fryer recipes on hand for unexpected changes

10. Incorporate Family Favourites:

   - Adapt family favourite recipes for the air fryer

   - This makes meal planning more appealing to everyone

11. Shop Smart:

   - Create your shopping list based on your meal plan

   - Buy ingredients that can be used in multiple air fryer recipes

12. Plan for Snacks:

   - Include air fryer snack recipes in your meal plan

   - This can help curb unhealthy snacking

Remember, the key to successful meal planning is finding a system that works for you and your lifestyle. Don't be afraid to adjust your approach as you go along. With your air fryer as a key tool, you'll find that preparing varied, healthy meals throughout the week becomes much more manageable.

BATCH COOKING WITH YOUR AIR FRYER OVEN

Batch cooking with your air fryer is a fantastic way to save time and ensure you have healthy, delicious meals ready throughout the week. Here's how to make the most of it:

1. Choose Versatile **Ingredients:**

   - Cook large batches of proteins like chicken breasts, meatballs, or tofu

   - Roast a variety of vegetables that can be used in multiple dishes

2. Maximize Space:

   - Use racks or separators to cook different foods simultaneously

   - Cook in layers if your air fryer allows it

3. Time It Right:

   - Start with foods that take longer to cook, then add quicker-cooking items

   - Use the pause function to add or remove items as needed

4. Prepare for the Week:

   - Dedicate a few hours on the weekend for batch cooking

   - Cook enough to last for 3-4 days (for food safety reasons)

5. Portion and Store Properly:

   - Divide cooked food into individual or family-sized portions

   - Use airtight containers or freezer bags for storage

6. Label Everything:

   - Note the contents and date of cooking on each container

   - This helps with meal planning and ensures food safety

7. Freeze Some Portions:

   - Many air fryer dishes freeze well for longer storage

   - Thaw in the fridge overnight before reheating

8. Plan for Variety:

   - Cook base ingredients that can be used in different ways (e.g., plain chicken for salads, stir-fries, or sandwiches)

9. Don't Forget Snacks:

   - Batch cook healthier snacks like kale chips or roasted chickpeas

10. Prep Raw **Ingredients:**

   - While batch cooking, prep raw ingredients for fresh meals later in the week

11. Use Recipe Multipliers:

   - Many recipes can be doubled or tripled for batch cooking

   - Adjust cooking times slightly for larger quantities

12. Clean As You Go:

   - Keep the process efficient by cleaning your air fryer between batches

Remember, not all foods are suitable for batch cooking. Focus on items that reheat well and can be used in various dishes.

WITH PRACTICE, YOU'LL DEVELOP A BATCH COOKING ROUTINE THAT WORKS BEST FOR YOU AND YOUR AIR FRYER, MAKING WEEKDAY MEALS A BREEZE.

STORAGE AND REHEATING TIPS

Proper storage and reheating are crucial for maintaining the quality and safety of your batch-cooked air fryer meals. Here are some tips I've found helpful:

STORAGE TIPS:

1. Cool Quickly:

   - Allow food to cool to room temperature before storing (but don't leave out for more than 2 hours)

   - Spread food out on a cool surface to speed up cooling

2. Use Appropriate Containers:

   - Opt for airtight, BPA-free containers

   - Glass containers are great for reheating in the microwave or oven

3. Portion Correctly:

   - Store in individual or family-sized portions for easy reheating

   - This also helps prevent waste

4. Label Everything:

   - Note the contents and date of cooking

   - Include reheating instructions if necessary

5. Refrigerate or Freeze:

   - Store meals you'll eat within 3-4 days in the fridge

   - Freeze meals for longer storage (up to 3 months for most foods)

6. Avoid Overpacking:

   - Leave some space in containers for air circulation in the fridge

   - For freezer storage, leave space for food expansion as it freezes

7. Store Components Separately:

   - Keep proteins, vegetables, and sauces in separate containers when possible

   - This allows for better reheating and more flexibility in meal assembly

REHEATING TIPS:

1. Use Your Air Fryer:

   - Great for restoring crispiness to fried or breaded items

   - Preheat to 180°C, then reheat for 3-5 minutes, shaking halfway through

2. Add Moisture:

   - Spritz dry foods with a little water before reheating to prevent drying out

3. Avoid Overcrowding:

   - Reheat in batches if necessary for even heating

4. Check Temperature:

   - Ensure reheated foods reach 74°C for food safety

5. Refresh with Seasonings:

   - Add a sprinkle of fresh herbs or a squeeze of lemon to brighten flavours

6. Use Other Methods When Appropriate:

   - Microwave for quick reheating of non-crispy items

   - Oven for larger portions that won't fit in the air fryer

7. Thaw Safely:

   - Move frozen meals to the fridge the night before for safe thawing

   - Some items can be reheated from frozen in the air fryer (adjust time accordingly)

8. Reheat Once:

   - For safety, only reheat meals once

9. Crisp Up Toppings:

   - Add fresh toppings after reheating for best texture (e.g., cheese, breadcrumbs)

10. Steam Method for Moisture:

   - For foods that tend to dry out, create a steam environment in your air fryer by adding a small oven-safe dish of water alongside the food

REMEMBER, DIFFERENT FOODS MAY REQUIRE DIFFERENT REHEATING METHODS. WITH PRACTICE, YOU'LL LEARN THE BEST WAYS TO STORE AND REHEAT YOUR FAVOURITE AIR FRYER DISHES WHILE MAINTAINING THEIR FLAVOUR AND TEXTURE.

PERFECT BACON

Prep: 5 mins | Cook: 10 mins | Serves: 4

Ingredients:

- US: 8 slices bacon, 2 tablespoons maple syrup (optional), 1 teaspoon black pepper (optional)
- UK: 8 rashers of bacon, 2 tablespoons maple syrup (optional), 1 teaspoon black pepper (optional)

Instructions:

1. Preheat your air fryer oven to 200°C (390°F).
2. Arrange the bacon slices in a single layer in the air fryer basket, ensuring they don't overlap.
3. Cook for 8-10 minutes, flipping halfway through using tongs, until crispy.
4. If desired, brush with maple syrup and sprinkle with black pepper before serving for a sweet and spicy twist.
5. Remove the bacon from the air fryer and place it on paper towels to drain excess fat.
6. Serve hot and enjoy your perfectly crispy bacon!

Nutritional Information:

- Calories: 150 | Fat: 12g | Carbs: 0g | Protein: 10g

FLUFFY FRENCH TOAST

Prep: 10 mins | Cook: 15 mins | Serves: 4

Ingredients:

- US: 4 slices bread, 2 eggs, 120ml milk, 1 teaspoon vanilla extract, 1 teaspoon cinnamon, 2 tablespoons butter
- UK: 4 slices bread, 2 eggs, 120ml milk, 1 teaspoon vanilla extract, 1 teaspoon cinnamon, 2 tablespoons butter

Instructions:

1. Preheat your air fryer oven to 180°C (350°F).
2. In a bowl, whisk together eggs, milk, vanilla extract, and cinnamon until well combined.
3. Dip each bread slice into the mixture, ensuring both sides are well-coated.
4. Place the coated bread slices in the air fryer basket in a single layer.
5. Cook for 8-10 minutes, flipping halfway through, until golden brown and fluffy.
6. Remove the French toast and spread with butter while still hot.
7. Serve with maple syrup, fresh berries, or a dusting of powdered sugar.

Nutritional Information:

- Calories: 220 | Fat: 10g | Carbs: 25g | Protein: 7g

BREAKFAST BURRITO

Prep: 15 mins | Cook: 10 mins | Serves: 4

Ingredients:

- US: 4 large tortillas, 200g cooked sausage (crumbled), 100g cheddar cheese (shredded), 4 eggs, 1 bell pepper (diced), 1 onion (diced), 2 tablespoons olive oil
- UK: 4 large tortillas, 200g cooked sausage (crumbled), 100g cheddar cheese (shredded), 4 eggs, 1 bell pepper (diced), 1 onion (diced), 2 tablespoons olive oil

Instructions:

1. Preheat your air fryer oven to 180°C (350°F).
2. In a pan, heat olive oil and sauté bell pepper and onion until soft.
3. Add eggs and cook, stirring constantly, until scrambled and fully cooked.
4. Lay out tortillas and evenly distribute the sausage, scrambled eggs, and cheese.
5. Roll up the tortillas tightly and place them in the air fryer basket.
6. Cook for 5-7 minutes, until the tortillas are crispy and the cheese is melted.
7. Serve hot with salsa or avocado slices.

Nutritional Information:

- Calories: 350 | Fat: 20g | Carbs: 25g | Protein: 15g

CRISPY HASH BROWNS

Prep: 10 mins | Cook: 15 mins | Serves: 4

Ingredients:

- US: 4 large potatoes (peeled and grated), 1 small onion (grated), 2 tablespoons flour, 1 egg, salt and pepper to taste, 2 tablespoons olive oil
- UK: 4 large potatoes (peeled and grated), 1 small onion (grated), 2 tablespoons flour, 1 egg, salt and pepper to taste, 2 tablespoons olive oil

Instructions:

1. Preheat your air fryer oven to 200°C (390°F).
2. In a bowl, combine grated potatoes, onion, flour, egg, salt, and pepper until well mixed.
3. Form the mixture into small patties.
4. Brush the patties with olive oil and place them in the air fryer basket.
5. Cook for 10-15 minutes, flipping halfway through, until golden brown and crispy.
6. Serve immediately with your favourite breakfast dishes.

Nutritional Information:

- Calories: 180 | Fat: 7g | Carbs: 25g | Protein: 4g

CHEESY EGG CUPS

Prep: 10 mins | Cook: 12 mins | Serves: 4

Ingredients:
- US: 6 large eggs, 100g cheddar cheese (shredded), 50g spinach (chopped), salt and pepper to taste, 2 tablespoons milk
- UK: 6 large eggs, 100g cheddar cheese (shredded), 50g spinach (chopped), salt and pepper to taste, 2 tablespoons milk

Instructions:
1. Preheat your air fryer oven to 180°C (350°F).
2. In a bowl, whisk together eggs, milk, salt, and pepper.
3. Add the cheese and spinach to the mixture and stir until well combined.
4. Pour the mixture into silicone muffin cups, filling each about three-quarters full.
5. Place the cups in the air fryer basket.
6. Cook for 10-12 minutes, until the egg cups are set and slightly golden on top.
7. Remove from the air fryer and let cool slightly before serving.
8. Serve warm as a delicious and easy breakfast option.

Nutritional Information:
- Calories: 150 | Fat: 10g | Carbs: 2g | Protein: 12g

CINNAMON ROLLS

Prep: 15 mins | Cook: 12 mins | Serves: 6

Ingredients:
- US: 1 can refrigerated cinnamon roll dough, 60g cream cheese (softened), 30g powdered sugar, 1 teaspoon vanilla extract
- UK: 1 can refrigerated cinnamon roll dough, 60g cream cheese (softened), 30g powdered sugar, 1 teaspoon vanilla extract

Instructions:
1. Preheat your air fryer oven to 180°C (350°F).
2. Arrange the cinnamon rolls in the air fryer basket, leaving space between each roll.
3. Cook for 10-12 minutes, until golden brown and cooked through.
4. While the rolls are cooking, mix the cream cheese, powdered sugar, and vanilla extract until smooth to make the icing.
5. Once the cinnamon rolls are done, remove them from the air fryer and let cool for a few minutes.
6. Drizzle the cream cheese icing over the warm rolls.
7. Serve immediately and enjoy the gooey, sweet treat.

Nutritional Information:
- Calories: 300 | Fat: 12g | Carbs: 42g | Protein: 5g

BREAKFAST SAUSAGE PATTIES

Ingredients:
- US: 500g ground pork, 1 teaspoon salt, 1 teaspoon black pepper, 1 teaspoon sage, 1/2 teaspoon thyme, 1/2 teaspoon paprika, 1/4 teaspoon garlic powder
- UK: 500g ground pork, 1 teaspoon salt, 1 teaspoon black pepper, 1 teaspoon sage, 1/2 teaspoon thyme, 1/2 teaspoon paprika, 1/4 teaspoon garlic powder

Instructions:
1. Preheat your air fryer oven to 190°C (375°F).
2. In a bowl, mix together the ground pork and all the spices until well combined.
3. Form the mixture into small patties.
4. Arrange the patties in the air fryer basket in a single layer.
5. Cook for 8-10 minutes, flipping halfway through, until the patties are cooked through and slightly crispy on the outside.
6. Remove from the air fryer and serve hot.

Nutritional Information:
- Calories: 220 | Fat: 18g | Carbs: 1g | Protein: 14g

GRANOLA

Prep: 10 mins | Cook: 15 mins | Serves: 6

Ingredients:
- US: 300g rolled oats, 100g nuts (chopped), 100g dried fruit (chopped), 60ml honey, 30ml olive oil, 1 teaspoon vanilla extract, 1 teaspoon cinnamon
- UK: 300g rolled oats, 100g nuts (chopped), 100g dried fruit (chopped), 60ml honey, 30ml olive oil, 1 teaspoon vanilla extract, 1 teaspoon cinnamon

Instructions:
1. Preheat your air fryer oven to 160°C (320°F).
2. In a bowl, combine oats, nuts, honey, olive oil, vanilla extract, and cinnamon. Mix well to coat all the ingredients.
3. Spread the mixture in a single layer in the air fryer basket.
4. Cook for 10-15 minutes, stirring occasionally, until golden brown and crisp.
5. Remove from the air fryer and let cool completely before adding the dried fruit.
6. Store in an airtight container and serve with yogurt or milk.

Nutritional Information:
- Calories: 250 | Fat: 12g | Carbs: 32g | Protein: 5g

FRUIT AND NUT BREAKFAST BAR

Prep: 15 mins | Cook: 20 mins | Serves: 8

Ingredients:

- US: 200g rolled oats, 100g mixed nuts (chopped), 100g dried fruit (chopped), 60ml honey, 60ml peanut butter, 1 teaspoon vanilla extract
- UK: 200g rolled oats, 100g mixed nuts (chopped), 100g dried fruit (chopped), 60ml honey, 60ml peanut butter, 1 teaspoon vanilla extract

Instructions:

1. Preheat your air fryer oven to 180°C (350°F).
2. In a bowl, combine oats, nuts, and dried fruit.
3. In a small saucepan, heat honey and peanut butter over low heat until melted and combined.
4. Pour the honey and peanut butter mixture over the dry ingredients and mix well.
5. Press the mixture firmly into a lined baking dish.
6. Place the dish in the air fryer oven and cook for 15-20 minutes, until set and golden brown.
7. Remove from the air fryer and let cool completely before cutting into bars.
8. Store in an airtight container for a quick and healthy breakfast on the go.

Nutritional Information:

- Calories: 280 | Fat: 15g | Carbs: 30g | Protein: 7g

BREAKFAST PIZZA

Prep: 15 mins | Cook: 10 mins | Serves: 4

Ingredients:

- US: 1 pizza dough, 4 eggs, 100g cheddar cheese (shredded), 50g cooked bacon (crumbled), 1 bell pepper (diced), 1 small onion (diced), salt and pepper to taste, 1 tablespoon olive oil
- UK: 1 pizza dough, 4 eggs, 100g cheddar cheese (shredded), 50g cooked bacon (crumbled), 1 bell pepper (diced), 1 small onion (diced), salt and pepper to taste, 1 tablespoon olive oil

Instructions:

1. Preheat your air fryer oven to 200°C (390°F).
2. Roll out the pizza dough and place it in the air fryer basket.
3. In a pan, heat olive oil and sauté bell pepper and onion until soft.
4. Spread the sautéed vegetables over the pizza dough.
5. Crack the eggs onto the dough, spacing them out evenly.
6. Sprinkle the cheese and crumbled bacon over the top.
7. Season with salt and pepper.
8. Cook for 8-10 minutes, until the crust is golden and the eggs are cooked to your liking.
9. Remove from the air fryer, slice, and serve hot.

Nutritional Information:

- Calories: 350 | Fat: 20g | Carbs: 25g | Protein: 15g

CRISPY CHICKEN WINGS

Prep: 10 mins | Cook: 25 mins | Serves: 4

Ingredients:

- US: 1kg chicken wings, 30ml olive oil, 1 teaspoon salt, 1 teaspoon black pepper, 1 teaspoon garlic powder, 1 teaspoon paprika
- UK: 1kg chicken wings, 30ml olive oil, 1 teaspoon salt, 1 teaspoon black pepper, 1 teaspoon garlic powder, 1 teaspoon paprika

Instructions:

1. Preheat your air fryer oven to 200°C (390°F).
2. In a large bowl, toss the chicken wings with olive oil, salt, black pepper, garlic powder, and paprika until evenly coated.
3. Arrange the wings in a single layer in the air fryer basket, ensuring they are not overcrowded.
4. Cook for 25 minutes, flipping halfway through, until the wings are golden brown and crispy.
5. Serve hot with your favourite dipping sauce.

Nutritional Information:

- Calories: 290 | Fat: 19g | Carbs: 2g | Protein: 27g

MOZZARELLA STICKS

Prep: 15 mins | Cook: 10 mins | Serves: 4

Ingredients:

- US: 200g mozzarella cheese (cut into sticks), 60g flour, 2 eggs (beaten), 120g breadcrumbs, 1 teaspoon Italian seasoning, salt, and pepper to taste
- UK: 200g mozzarella cheese (cut into sticks), 60g flour, 2 eggs (beaten), 120g breadcrumbs, 1 teaspoon Italian seasoning, salt, and pepper to taste

Instructions:

1. Preheat your air fryer oven to 180°C (350°F).
2. Coat the mozzarella sticks first in flour, then dip in beaten eggs, and finally coat with breadcrumbs mixed with Italian seasoning, salt, and pepper.
3. Place the breaded mozzarella sticks in the air fryer basket in a single layer.
4. Cook for 8-10 minutes, or until golden and crispy.
5. Serve immediately with marinara sauce.

Nutritional Information:

- Calories: 250 | Fat: 15g | Carbs: 20g | Protein: 10g

LOADED POTATO SKINS

Prep: 10 mins | Cook: 20 mins | Serves: 4

Ingredients:

- US: 4 large potatoes, 100g cheddar cheese (shredded), 50g bacon bits, 2 spring onions (sliced), 60ml sour cream, 30ml olive oil, salt and pepper to taste
- UK: 4 large potatoes, 100g cheddar cheese (shredded), 50g bacon bits, 2 spring onions (sliced), 60ml sour cream, 30ml olive oil, salt and pepper to taste

Instructions:

1. Preheat your air fryer oven to 200°C (390°F).
2. Cut the potatoes in half and scoop out most of the flesh, leaving a small amount to support the skin.
3. Brush the potato skins with olive oil and season with salt and pepper.
4. Place the skins in the air fryer basket and cook for 10 minutes.
5. Remove the skins, sprinkle with cheese and bacon bits, and return to the air fryer for another 5-7 minutes until the cheese is melted and bubbly.
6. Top with sliced spring onions and a dollop of sour cream before serving.

Nutritional Information:

- Calories: 350 | Fat: 18g | Carbs: 35g | Protein: 12g

HOMEMADE CRISPS

Prep: 10 mins | Cook: 15 mins | Serves: 4

Ingredients:

- US: 4 large potatoes (thinly sliced), 30ml olive oil, salt and pepper to taste
- UK: 4 large potatoes (thinly sliced), 30ml olive oil, salt and pepper to taste

Instructions:

1. Preheat your air fryer oven to 180°C (350°F).
2. In a bowl, toss the potato slices with olive oil, salt, and pepper.
3. Arrange the slices in a single layer in the air fryer basket.
4. Cook for 12-15 minutes, shaking the basket halfway through, until the crisps are golden brown and crispy.
5. Remove and let cool slightly before serving.

Nutritional Information:

- Calories: 200 | Fat: 8g | Carbs: 30g | Protein: 3g

GARLIC PARMESAN MUSHROOMS

Prep: 10 mins | Cook: 15 mins | Serves: 4

Ingredients:

- US: 400g button mushrooms, 30ml olive oil, 30g grated Parmesan cheese, 1 teaspoon garlic powder, salt and pepper to taste, chopped fresh parsley for garnish
- UK: 400g button mushrooms, 30ml olive oil, 30g grated Parmesan cheese, 1 teaspoon garlic powder, salt and pepper to taste, chopped fresh parsley for garnish

Instructions:

1. Preheat your air fryer oven to 180°C (350°F).
2. In a bowl, toss the mushrooms with olive oil, Parmesan cheese, garlic powder, salt, and pepper.
3. Arrange the mushrooms in a single layer in the air fryer basket.
4. Cook for 12-15 minutes, shaking the basket halfway through, until the mushrooms are tender and golden.
5. Garnish with chopped parsley and serve immediately.

Nutritional Information:

- Calories: 120 | Fat: 9g | Carbs: 5g | Protein: 4g

SPINACH AND ARTICHOKE DIP

Prep: 15 mins | Cook: 10 mins | Serves: 4

Ingredients:

- US: 200g spinach (fresh or frozen, thawed and drained), 200g artichoke hearts (chopped), 100g cream cheese, 50g sour cream, 50g mayonnaise, 50g grated Parmesan cheese, 1 teaspoon garlic powder, salt and pepper to taste
- UK: 200g spinach (fresh or frozen, thawed and drained), 200g artichoke hearts (chopped), 100g cream cheese, 50g sour cream, 50g mayonnaise, 50g grated Parmesan cheese, 1 teaspoon garlic powder, salt and pepper to taste

Instructions:

1. Preheat your air fryer oven to 180°C (350°F).
2. In a bowl, mix together spinach, artichoke hearts, cream cheese, sour cream, mayonnaise, Parmesan cheese, garlic powder, salt, and pepper until well combined.
3. Transfer the mixture to a baking dish that fits your air fryer oven.
4. Cook for 10 minutes, or until the dip is hot and bubbly.
5. Serve warm with tortilla chips or bread slices.

Nutritional Information:

- Calories: 210 | Fat: 18g | Carbs: 6g | Protein: 6g

ONION BHAJIS

Prep: 15 mins | Cook: 10 mins | Serves: 4

Ingredients:
- US: 2 large onions (thinly sliced), 150g chickpea flour, 1 teaspoon turmeric, 1 teaspoon cumin, 1 teaspoon coriander, 1 teaspoon salt, 30ml water, 30ml vegetable oil
- UK: 2 large onions (thinly sliced), 150g chickpea flour, 1 teaspoon turmeric, 1 teaspoon cumin, 1 teaspoon coriander, 1 teaspoon salt, 30ml water, 30ml vegetable oil

Instructions:
1. Preheat your air fryer oven to 180°C (350°F).
2. In a bowl, mix together chickpea flour, turmeric, cumin, coriander, and salt.
3. Gradually add water to the mixture, stirring until a thick batter forms.
4. Add the sliced onions and mix until they are well-coated with the batter.
5. Form small fritters and place them in the air fryer basket.
6. Brush or spray the fritters with vegetable oil.
7. Cook for 10 minutes, flipping halfway through, until golden and crispy.
8. Serve hot with chutney or raita.

Nutritional Information:
- Calories: 150 | Fat: 7g | Carbs: 20g | Protein: 3g

CRISPY TOFU BITES

Prep: 15 mins | Cook: 20 mins | Serves: 4

Ingredients:
- US: 400g firm tofu (cubed), 30ml soy sauce, 15ml sesame oil, 2 tablespoons cornstarch, 1 teaspoon garlic powder, 1 teaspoon paprika, salt and pepper to taste
- UK: 400g firm tofu (cubed), 30ml soy sauce, 15ml sesame oil, 2 tablespoons cornstarch, 1 teaspoon garlic powder, 1 teaspoon paprika, salt and pepper to taste

Instructions:
1. Preheat your air fryer oven to 200°C (390°F).
2. In a bowl, marinate the tofu cubes with soy sauce and sesame oil for 10 minutes.
3. In a separate bowl, mix together cornstarch, garlic powder, paprika, salt, and pepper.
4. Toss the marinated tofu cubes in the cornstarch mixture until evenly coated.
5. Place the tofu cubes in the air fryer basket in a single layer.
6. Cook for 15-20 minutes, shaking the basket halfway through, until the tofu is crispy and golden.
7. Serve with a dipping sauce of your choice.

Nutritional Information:
- Calories: 180 | Fat: 10g | Carbs: 10g | Protein: 12g

STUFFED JALAPEÑO POPPERS

Prep: 15 mins | Cook: 10 mins | Serves: 4

Ingredients:

- US: 12 large jalapeños, 100g cream cheese, 50g cheddar cheese (shredded), 50g bacon bits, 1 teaspoon garlic powder, salt and pepper to taste
- UK: 12 large jalapeños, 100g cream cheese, 50g cheddar cheese (shredded), 50g bacon bits, 1 teaspoon garlic powder, salt and pepper to taste

Instructions:

1. Preheat your air fryer oven to 180°C (350°F).
2. Cut the jalapeños in half lengthwise and remove the seeds.
3. In a bowl, mix together cream cheese, cheddar cheese, bacon bits, garlic powder, salt, and pepper.
4. Stuff each jalapeño half with the cheese mixture.
5. Place the stuffed jalapeños in the air fryer basket in a single layer.
6. Cook for 8-10 minutes, until the jalapeños are tender and the cheese is melted and bubbly.
7. Serve immediately.

Nutritional Information:

- Calories: 150 | Fat: 12g | Carbs: 5g | Protein: 5g

SWEET POTATO WEDGES

Prep: 10 mins | Cook: 20 mins | Serves: 4

Ingredients:

- US: 4 large sweet potatoes (cut into wedges), 30ml olive oil, 1 teaspoon paprika, 1 teaspoon garlic powder, salt and pepper to taste
- UK: 4 large sweet potatoes (cut into wedges), 30ml olive oil, 1 teaspoon paprika, 1 teaspoon garlic powder, salt and pepper to taste

Instructions:

1. Preheat your air fryer oven to 200°C (390°F).
2. In a bowl, toss the sweet potato wedges with olive oil, paprika, garlic powder, salt, and pepper until evenly coated.
3. Arrange the wedges in a single layer in the air fryer basket.
4. Cook for 15-20 minutes, shaking the basket halfway through, until the wedges are crispy on the outside and tender on the inside.
5. Serve hot, optionally with a dipping sauce.

Nutritional Information:

- Calories: 220 | Fat: 7g | Carbs: 36g | Protein: 2g

VEGETABLE SIDES

ROASTED BROCCOLI

Prep: 5 mins | Cook: 12 mins | Serves: 4

Ingredients:

- US: 500g broccoli florets, 2 tablespoons olive oil, 1 teaspoon garlic powder, 1 teaspoon salt, 1 teaspoon black pepper
- UK: 500g broccoli florets, 2 tablespoons olive oil, 1 teaspoon garlic powder, 1 teaspoon salt, 1 teaspoon black pepper

Instructions:

1. Preheat your air fryer oven to 200°C (390°F).
2. In a bowl, toss the broccoli florets with olive oil, garlic powder, salt, and pepper.
3. Spread the broccoli in a single layer in the air fryer basket.
4. Cook for 10-12 minutes, shaking the basket halfway through, until the broccoli is tender and slightly crispy.
5. Serve hot and enjoy your delicious roasted broccoli!

Nutritional Information:

- Calories: 120 | Fat: 7g | Carbs: 12g | Protein: 4g

CRISPY BRUSSELS SPROUTS

Prep: 10 mins | Cook: 15 mins | Serves: 4

Ingredients:

- US: 500g Brussels sprouts (halved), 2 tablespoons olive oil, 1 teaspoon salt, 1 teaspoon black pepper, 1 tablespoon balsamic vinegar
- UK: 500g Brussels sprouts (halved), 2 tablespoons olive oil, 1 teaspoon salt, 1 teaspoon black pepper, 1 tablespoon balsamic vinegar

Instructions:

1. Preheat your air fryer oven to 190°C (375°F).
2. In a bowl, toss the halved Brussels sprouts with olive oil, salt, and pepper.
3. Place the Brussels sprouts in the air fryer basket in a single layer.
4. Cook for 12-15 minutes, shaking the basket halfway through, until crispy and golden brown.
5. Drizzle with balsamic vinegar before serving.

Nutritional Information:

- Calories: 140 | Fat: 8g | Carbs: 15g | Protein: 4g

HONEY-GLAZED CARROTS

Prep: 10 mins | Cook: 15 mins | Serves: 4

Ingredients:

- US: 500g carrots (peeled and sliced into sticks), 30ml olive oil, 2 tablespoons honey, 1 tablespoon balsamic vinegar, salt, pepper, chopped fresh parsley (for garnish)
- UK: 500g carrots (peeled and sliced into sticks), 30ml olive oil, 2 tablespoons honey, 1 tablespoon balsamic vinegar, salt, pepper, chopped fresh parsley (for garnish)

Instructions:

1. Preheat your air fryer oven to 200°C (390°F).
2. In a bowl, toss the carrot sticks with olive oil, honey, balsamic vinegar, salt, and pepper until well coated.
3. Spread the glazed carrots in a single layer in the air fryer basket.
4. Cook for about 10-15 minutes, shaking the basket occasionally, until the carrots are tender and caramelized.
5. Garnish with chopped fresh parsley before serving.

Nutritional Information:

- Calories: 130 | Fat: 7g | Carbs: 18g | Protein: 1g

GARLIC GREEN BEANS

Prep: 5 mins | Cook: 10 mins | Serves: 4

Ingredients:

- US: 500g green beans (trimmed), 2 tablespoons olive oil, 3 garlic cloves (minced), 1 teaspoon salt, 1 teaspoon black pepper
- UK: 500g green beans (trimmed), 2 tablespoons olive oil, 3 garlic cloves (minced), 1 teaspoon salt, 1 teaspoon black pepper

Instructions:

1. Preheat your air fryer oven to 190°C (375°F).
2. In a bowl, toss the green beans with olive oil, minced garlic, salt, and pepper.
3. Place the green beans in the air fryer basket in a single layer.
4. Cook for 8-10 minutes, shaking the basket halfway through, until the beans are tender and slightly crispy.
5. Serve immediately.

Nutritional Information:

- Calories: 110 | Fat: 7g | Carbs: 10g | Protein: 2g

PARMESAN ZUCCHINI CHIPS

Prep: 10 mins | Cook: 15 mins | Serves: 4

Ingredients:

- US: 2 large zucchinis (sliced into thin rounds), 50g grated Parmesan cheese, 2 tablespoons olive oil, 1 teaspoon garlic powder, salt, and pepper to taste
- UK: 2 large courgettes (sliced into thin rounds), 50g grated Parmesan cheese, 2 tablespoons olive oil, 1 teaspoon garlic powder, salt, and pepper to taste

Instructions:

1. Preheat your air fryer oven to 200°C (390°F).
2. In a bowl, toss the zucchini slices with olive oil, Parmesan cheese, garlic powder, salt, and pepper.
3. Place the zucchini slices in a single layer in the air fryer basket.
4. Cook for 12-15 minutes, flipping halfway through, until golden brown and crispy.
5. Serve as a delicious and healthy snack or side dish.

Nutritional Information:

- Calories: 150 | Fat: 10g | Carbs: 7g | Protein: 6g

SPICY CAULIFLOWER BITES

Prep: 10 mins | Cook: 20 mins | Serves: 4

Ingredients:

- US: 500g cauliflower florets, 2 tablespoons olive oil, 1 tablespoon hot sauce, 1 teaspoon garlic powder, 1 teaspoon paprika, salt to taste
- UK: 500g cauliflower florets, 2 tablespoons olive oil, 1 tablespoon hot sauce, 1 teaspoon garlic powder, 1 teaspoon paprika, salt to taste

Instructions:

1. Preheat your air fryer oven to 200°C (390°F).
2. In a bowl, toss the cauliflower florets with olive oil, hot sauce, garlic powder, paprika, and salt.
3. Spread the cauliflower in a single layer in the air fryer basket.
4. Cook for 18-20 minutes, shaking the basket halfway through, until the cauliflower is tender and slightly crispy.
5. Serve hot as a spicy and tasty side dish or snack.

Nutritional Information:

- Calories: 130 | Fat: 7g | Carbs: 14g | Protein: 3g

STUFFED BELL PEPPERS

Prep: 15 mins | Cook: 20 mins | Serves: 4

Ingredients:

- US: 4 bell peppers (halved and seeded), 250g cooked rice, 200g ground beef, 1 onion (diced), 1 can diced tomatoes, 1 teaspoon garlic powder, 1 teaspoon salt, 1 teaspoon black pepper, 50g shredded cheese
- UK: 4 bell peppers (halved and seeded), 250g cooked rice, 200g minced beef, 1 onion (diced), 1 can diced tomatoes, 1 teaspoon garlic powder, 1 teaspoon salt, 1 teaspoon black pepper, 50g shredded cheese

Instructions:

1. Preheat your air fryer oven to 180°C (350°F).
2. In a pan, cook the ground beef and diced onion until browned.
3. Add the cooked rice, diced tomatoes, garlic powder, salt, and pepper to the pan and mix well.
4. Stuff each bell pepper half with the mixture and top with shredded cheese.
5. Place the stuffed peppers in the air fryer basket and cook for 15-20 minutes, until the peppers are tender and the cheese is melted and bubbly.
6. Serve hot as a hearty and satisfying main dish.

Nutritional Information:

- Calories: 220 | Fat: 10g | Carbs: 22g | Protein: 10g

CRISPY KALE CHIPS

Prep: 5 mins | Cook: 10 mins | Serves: 4

Ingredients:

- US: 200g kale leaves (stems removed and torn into pieces), 2 tablespoons olive oil, 1 teaspoon salt, 1 teaspoon garlic powder
- UK: 200g kale leaves (stems removed and torn into pieces), 2 tablespoons olive oil, 1 teaspoon salt, 1 teaspoon garlic powder

Instructions:

1. Preheat your air fryer oven to 150°C (300°F).
2. In a bowl, toss the kale leaves with olive oil, salt, and garlic powder.
3. Spread the kale in a single layer in the air fryer basket.
4. Cook for 8-10 minutes, shaking the basket halfway through, until the kale is crispy and slightly browned.
5. Serve immediately as a light and healthy snack.

Nutritional Information:

- Calories: 80 | Fat: 7g | Carbs: 4g | Protein: 2g

HERB-ROASTED CHERRY TOMATOES

Prep: 5 mins | Cook: 10 mins | Serves: 4

Ingredients:

- US: 500g cherry tomatoes, 2 tablespoons olive oil, 1 teaspoon dried oregano, 1 teaspoon dried basil, salt and pepper to taste
- UK: 500g cherry tomatoes, 2 tablespoons olive oil, 1 teaspoon dried oregano, 1 teaspoon dried basil, salt and pepper to taste

Instructions:

1. Preheat your air fryer oven to 200°C (390°F).
2. In a bowl, toss the cherry tomatoes with olive oil, oregano, basil, salt, and pepper.
3. Spread the tomatoes in a single layer in the air fryer basket.
4. Cook for 8-10 minutes, shaking the basket halfway through, until the tomatoes are soft and slightly blistered.
5. Serve as a delightful side dish or add to salads and pasta.

Nutritional Information:

- Calories: 90 | Fat: 7g | Carbs: 6g | Protein: 1g

BUTTERNUT SQUASH CUBES

Prep: 10 mins | Cook: 20 mins | Serves: 4

Ingredients:

- US: 500g butternut squash (peeled and cubed), 2 tablespoons olive oil, 1 teaspoon cinnamon, 1 teaspoon salt, 1 tablespoon maple syrup
- UK: 500g butternut squash (peeled and cubed), 2 tablespoons olive oil, 1 teaspoon cinnamon, 1 teaspoon salt, 1 tablespoon maple syrup

Instructions:

1. Preheat your air fryer oven to 200°C (390°F).
2. In a bowl, toss the butternut squash cubes with olive oil, cinnamon, salt, and maple syrup.
3. Spread the squash in a single layer in the air fryer basket.
4. Cook for 18-20 minutes, shaking the basket halfway through, until the squash is tender and caramelized.
5. Serve as a sweet and savoury side dish that's perfect for any meal.

Nutritional Information:

- Calories: 140 | Fat: 7g | Carbs: 20g | Protein: 1g

POTATO PERFECTION

CLASSIC CHIPS

Prep: 10 mins | Cook: 20 mins | Serves: 4

Ingredients:

- US: 1kg potatoes (cut into thin strips), 30ml olive oil, 1 teaspoon salt, 1/2 teaspoon black pepper
- UK: 1kg potatoes (cut into thin strips), 30ml olive oil, 1 teaspoon salt, 1/2 teaspoon black pepper

Instructions:

1. Preheat your air fryer oven to 200°C (390°F).
2. In a bowl, toss the potato strips with olive oil, salt, and black pepper until evenly coated.
3. Place the chips in the air fryer basket in a single layer.
4. Cook for 15-20 minutes, shaking the basket halfway through, until golden and crispy.
5. Serve hot with your favourite dipping sauce.

Nutritional Information:

- Calories: 200 | Fat: 7g | Carbs: 30g | Protein: 3g

HASSELBACK POTATOES

Prep: 10 mins | Cook: 25 mins | Serves: 4

Ingredients:

- US: 4 medium potatoes, 30ml olive oil, 1 teaspoon salt, 1 teaspoon garlic powder, 1 teaspoon dried rosemary
- UK: 4 medium potatoes, 30ml olive oil, 1 teaspoon salt, 1 teaspoon garlic powder, 1 teaspoon dried rosemary

Instructions:

1. Preheat your air fryer oven to 200°C (390°F).
2. Make thin slices across each potato, stopping just before cutting through.
3. In a bowl, mix olive oil, salt, garlic powder, and dried rosemary.
4. Brush the oil mixture over the potatoes, making sure it seeps into the cuts.
5. Place the potatoes in the air fryer basket and cook for 25 minutes, until tender and crispy.
6. Serve hot as a perfect side dish.

Nutritional Information:

- Calories: 180 | Fat: 8g | Carbs: 25g | Protein: 3g

LOADED POTATO WEDGES

Prep: 10 mins | Cook: 20 mins | Serves: 4

Ingredients:

- US: 1kg potatoes (cut into wedges), 30ml olive oil, 1 teaspoon paprika, 1 teaspoon garlic powder, 1 teaspoon salt, 100g shredded cheddar cheese, 50g cooked bacon bits, 2 tablespoons chopped chives
- UK: 1kg potatoes (cut into wedges), 30ml olive oil, 1 teaspoon paprika, 1 teaspoon garlic powder, 1 teaspoon salt, 100g shredded cheddar cheese, 50g cooked bacon bits, 2 tablespoons chopped chives

Instructions:

1. Preheat your air fryer oven to 200°C (390°F).
2. In a bowl, toss the potato wedges with olive oil, paprika, garlic powder, and salt.
3. Place the wedges in the air fryer basket in a single layer.
4. Cook for 15 minutes, shaking halfway through.
5. Sprinkle cheese and bacon bits over the wedges and cook for another 5 minutes until the cheese is melted.
6. Garnish with chopped chives and serve hot.

Nutritional Information:

- Calories: 350 | Fat: 18g | Carbs: 35g | Protein: 12g

CRISPY ROAST POTATOES

Prep: 10 mins | Cook: 25 mins | Serves: 4

Ingredients:

- US: 1kg baby potatoes (halved), 30ml olive oil, 1 teaspoon salt, 1 teaspoon dried thyme
- UK: 1kg baby potatoes (halved), 30ml olive oil, 1 teaspoon salt, 1 teaspoon dried thyme

Instructions:

1. Preheat your air fryer oven to 200°C (390°F).
2. In a bowl, toss the halved potatoes with olive oil, salt, and dried thyme.
3. Place the potatoes in the air fryer basket in a single layer.
4. Cook for 20-25 minutes, shaking halfway through, until golden and crispy.
5. Serve hot as a delicious side dish.

Nutritional Information:

- Calories: 200 | Fat: 7g | Carbs: 30g | Protein: 3g

SWEET POTATO FRIES

Prep: 10 mins | Cook: 20 mins | Serves: 4

Ingredients:

- US: 1kg sweet potatoes (cut into thin strips), 30ml olive oil, 1 teaspoon salt, 1/2 teaspoon cinnamon (optional)
- UK: 1kg sweet potatoes (cut into thin strips), 30ml olive oil, 1 teaspoon salt, 1/2 teaspoon cinnamon (optional)

Instructions:

1. Preheat your air fryer oven to 200°C (390°F).
2. In a bowl, toss the sweet potato strips with olive oil, salt, and cinnamon if using.
3. Place the fries in the air fryer basket in a single layer.
4. Cook for 15-20 minutes, shaking halfway through, until golden and crispy.
5. Serve hot with your favourite dipping sauce.

Nutritional Information:

- Calories: 250 | Fat: 7g | Carbs: 45g | Protein: 2g

POTATO CROQUETTES

Prep: 15 mins | Cook: 15 mins | Serves: 4

Ingredients:

- US: 500g mashed potatoes, 100g grated cheese, 1 egg, 50g breadcrumbs, salt, and pepper to taste, 2 tablespoons olive oil
- UK: 500g mashed potatoes, 100g grated cheese, 1 egg, 50g breadcrumbs, salt, and pepper to taste, 2 tablespoons olive oil

Instructions:

1. Preheat your air fryer oven to 200°C (390°F).
2. In a bowl, mix mashed potatoes, cheese, egg, salt, and pepper until well combined.
3. Shape the mixture into small balls and roll in breadcrumbs.
4. Brush with olive oil and place in the air fryer basket.
5. Cook for 12-15 minutes, shaking halfway through, until golden and crispy.
6. Serve hot as a snack or side dish.

Nutritional Information:

- Calories: 220 | Fat: 10g | Carbs: 25g | Protein: 7g

TWICE-BAKED POTATOES

Prep: 15 mins | Cook: 30 mins | Serves: 4

Ingredients:

- US: 4 large potatoes, 50g butter, 100ml sour cream, 100g grated cheese, 50g bacon bits, salt, and pepper to taste, 2 tablespoons chopped chives
- UK: 4 large potatoes, 50g butter, 100ml sour cream, 100g grated cheese, 50g bacon bits, salt, and pepper to taste, 2 tablespoons chopped chives

Instructions:

1. Preheat your air fryer oven to 200°C (390°F).
2. Bake the potatoes for 20 minutes until tender.
3. Cut the potatoes in half and scoop out the flesh, leaving a thin layer.
4. In a bowl, mix the potato flesh with butter, sour cream, cheese, bacon bits, salt, and pepper.
5. Fill the potato skins with the mixture and return to the air fryer.
6. Bake for another 10 minutes until golden and bubbly.
7. Garnish with chopped chives and serve hot.

Nutritional Information:

- Calories: 300 | Fat: 15g | Carbs: 35g | Protein: 8g

POTATO SKINS

Prep: 10 mins | Cook: 20 mins | Serves: 4

Ingredients:

- US: 4 large potatoes, 30ml olive oil, 100g shredded cheese, 50g bacon bits, 2 tablespoons sour cream, 2 tablespoons chopped chives, salt, and pepper to taste
- UK: 4 large potatoes, 30ml olive oil, 100g shredded cheese, 50g bacon bits, 2 tablespoons sour cream, 2 tablespoons chopped chives, salt, and pepper to taste

Instructions:

1. Preheat your air fryer oven to 200°C (390°F).
2. Bake the potatoes for 20 minutes until tender.
3. Cut the potatoes in half and scoop out most of the flesh, leaving a thin layer.
4. Brush the skins with olive oil and season with salt and pepper.
5. Place the skins in the air fryer basket and cook for 10 minutes until crispy.
6. Fill each skin with cheese and bacon bits, then cook for another 5 minutes until the cheese is melted.
7. Top with sour cream and chopped chives.
8. Serve hot as an appetiser or snack.

Nutritional Information:

- Calories: 280 | Fat: 12g | Carbs: 35g | Protein: 8g

GARLIC PARMESAN POTATO CUBES

Prep: 10 mins | Cook: 20 mins | Serves: 4

Ingredients:

- US: 1kg potatoes (cut into cubes), 30ml olive oil, 1 teaspoon garlic powder, 50g grated Parmesan cheese, 1 teaspoon salt, 1 teaspoon dried parsley
- UK: 1kg potatoes (cut into cubes), 30ml olive oil, 1 teaspoon garlic powder, 50g grated Parmesan cheese, 1 teaspoon salt, 1 teaspoon dried parsley

Instructions:

1. Preheat your air fryer oven to 200°C (390°F).
2. In a bowl, toss the potato cubes with olive oil, garlic powder, Parmesan cheese, salt, and dried parsley.
3. Place the cubes in the air fryer basket in a single layer.
4. Cook for 15-20 minutes, shaking halfway through, until golden and crispy.
5. Serve hot as a delicious side dish.

Nutritional Information:

- Calories: 220 | Fat: 8g | Carbs: 30g | Protein: 5g

CRISPY SMASHED POTATOES

Prep: 10 mins | Cook: 25 mins | Serves: 4

Ingredients:

- US: 1kg baby potatoes, 30ml olive oil, 1 teaspoon salt, 1 teaspoon garlic powder, 1 teaspoon dried rosemary
- UK: 1kg baby potatoes, 30ml olive oil, 1 teaspoon salt, 1 teaspoon garlic powder, 1 teaspoon dried rosemary

Instructions:

1. Preheat your air fryer oven to 200°C (390°F).
2. Boil the potatoes for 10 minutes until tender.
3. Drain and gently smash each potato with a fork.
4. In a bowl, toss the smashed potatoes with olive oil, salt, garlic powder, and dried rosemary.
5. Place the potatoes in the air fryer basket in a single layer.
6. Cook for 15 minutes until golden and crispy.
7. Serve hot as a tasty side dish.

Nutritional Information:

- Calories: 200 | Fat: 7g | Carbs: 30g | Protein: 3g

CRISPY CHICKEN TENDERS

Prep: 10 mins | Cook: 15 mins | Serves: 4

Ingredients:

- US: 500g chicken tenders, 100g plain flour, 2 eggs (beaten), 100g breadcrumbs, 1 teaspoon garlic powder, 1 teaspoon paprika, salt and pepper to taste, 30ml olive oil
- UK: 500g chicken tenders, 100g plain flour, 2 eggs (beaten), 100g breadcrumbs, 1 teaspoon garlic powder, 1 teaspoon paprika, salt and pepper to taste, 30ml olive oil

Instructions:

1. Preheat your air fryer oven to 200°C (390°F).
2. Season the flour with garlic powder, paprika, salt, and pepper.
3. Coat the chicken tenders in the seasoned flour, dip into the beaten eggs, and then coat with breadcrumbs.
4. Lightly spray or brush the tenders with olive oil.
5. Arrange the chicken tenders in a single layer in the air fryer basket.
6. Cook for 10-15 minutes, turning halfway through, until golden brown and crispy.
7. Serve with your favourite dipping sauce.

Nutritional Information:

- Calories: 290 | Fat: 12g | Carbs: 20g | Protein: 25g

CHICKEN FAJITAS

Prep: 10 mins | Cook: 15 mins | Serves: 4

Ingredients:

- US: 500g chicken breast (sliced), 1 bell pepper (sliced), 1 onion (sliced), 2 tablespoons olive oil, 1 teaspoon chili powder, 1 teaspoon cumin, 1 teaspoon paprika, salt and pepper to taste, 4 tortillas
- UK: 500g chicken breast (sliced), 1 bell pepper (sliced), 1 onion (sliced), 2 tablespoons olive oil, 1 teaspoon chili powder, 1 teaspoon cumin, 1 teaspoon paprika, salt and pepper to taste, 4 tortillas

Instructions:

1. Preheat your air fryer oven to 200°C (390°F).
2. In a bowl, mix the chicken, bell pepper, onion, olive oil, chili powder, cumin, paprika, salt, and pepper.
3. Place the mixture in the air fryer basket in a single layer.
4. Cook for 10-15 minutes, shaking the basket halfway through, until the chicken is cooked and the vegetables are tender.
5. Serve the fajita mixture in tortillas with your favourite toppings.

Nutritional Information:

- Calories: 350 | Fat: 15g | Carbs: 30g | Protein: 20g

LEMON HERB CHICKEN BREASTS

Prep: 10 mins | Cook: 20 mins | Serves: 4

Ingredients:

- US: 4 chicken breasts (about 150g each), 60ml olive oil, juice of 1 lemon, 2 tablespoons dried oregano, 2 tablespoons dried thyme, 2 garlic cloves (minced), salt and pepper to taste
- UK: 4 chicken breasts (about 150g each), 60ml olive oil, juice of 1 lemon, 2 tablespoons dried oregano, 2 tablespoons dried thyme, 2 garlic cloves (minced), salt and pepper to taste

Instructions:

1. Preheat your air fryer oven to 200°C (390°F).
2. In a bowl, mix olive oil, lemon juice, oregano, thyme, garlic, salt, and pepper.
3. Coat the chicken breasts in the marinade and let sit for 10 minutes.
4. Place the chicken breasts in the air fryer basket.
5. Cook for 15-20 minutes, turning halfway through, until the chicken is cooked through and juices run clear.
6. Serve with a fresh salad or steamed vegetables.

Nutritional Information:

- Calories: 220 | Fat: 10g | Carbs: 2g | Protein: 30g

HONEY MUSTARD CHICKEN THIGHS

Prep: 10 mins | Cook: 25 mins | Serves: 4

Ingredients:

- US: 8 chicken thighs, 60ml honey, 60ml Dijon mustard, 2 tablespoons olive oil, 1 tablespoon apple cider vinegar, salt and pepper to taste
- UK: 8 chicken thighs, 60ml honey, 60ml Dijon mustard, 2 tablespoons olive oil, 1 tablespoon apple cider vinegar, salt and pepper to taste

Instructions:

1. Preheat your air fryer oven to 200°C (390°F).
2. In a bowl, whisk together honey, Dijon mustard, olive oil, apple cider vinegar, salt, and pepper.
3. Coat the chicken thighs in the honey mustard mixture.
4. Place the chicken thighs in the air fryer basket in a single layer.
5. Cook for 20-25 minutes, turning halfway through, until the chicken is cooked through and the skin is crispy.
6. Serve with rice or roasted vegetables.

Nutritional Information:

- Calories: 310 | Fat: 18g | Carbs: 15g | Protein: 22g

JUICY WHOLE CHICKEN

Prep: 15 mins | Cook: 1 hour 30 mins | Serves: 4-6

Ingredients:

- US: 1 whole chicken (about 1.5kg), 60ml olive oil, 2 tablespoons garlic powder, 2 tablespoons paprika, 1 tablespoon dried thyme, 1 tablespoon dried rosemary, 1 teaspoon salt, 1 teaspoon black pepper, 1 lemon (quartered)
- UK: 1 whole chicken (about 1.5kg), 60ml olive oil, 2 tablespoons garlic powder, 2 tablespoons paprika, 1 tablespoon dried thyme, 1 tablespoon dried rosemary, 1 teaspoon salt, 1 teaspoon black pepper, 1 lemon (quartered)

Instructions:

1. Preheat your air fryer oven to 180°C (350°F).
2. In a small bowl, mix together the olive oil, garlic powder, paprika, thyme, rosemary, salt, and pepper.
3. Rub the seasoning mixture all over the chicken, including under the skin.
4. Stuff the lemon quarters inside the cavity of the chicken.
5. Place the chicken breast-side down in the air fryer basket.
6. Cook for 45 minutes, then carefully flip the chicken over.
7. Continue cooking for another 45 minutes, or until the internal temperature reaches 75°C (165°F) and the juices run clear.
8. Let the chicken rest for 10 minutes before carving.
9. Serve with your favourite sides.

Nutritional Information:

- Calories: 320 | Fat: 22g | Carbs: 2g | Protein: 27g

DUCK BREAST WITH CRISPY SKIN

Prep: 10 mins | Cook: 20 mins | Serves: 2

Ingredients:

- US: 2 duck breasts, 1 teaspoon salt, 1 teaspoon black pepper, 1 tablespoon olive oil
- UK: 2 duck breasts, 1 teaspoon salt, 1 teaspoon black pepper, 1 tablespoon olive oil

Instructions:

1. Preheat your air fryer oven to 200°C (390°F).
2. Score the skin of the duck breasts in a crisscross pattern, being careful not to cut into the meat.
3. Season both sides of the duck breasts with salt and pepper.
4. Rub the skin side with olive oil.
5. Place the duck breasts skin-side down in the air fryer basket.
6. Cook for 10 minutes, then flip and cook for another 10 minutes, or until the internal temperature reaches 60°C (140°F) for medium-rare.
7. Let the duck rest for 5 minutes before slicing.
8. Serve with a fruit sauce and roasted vegetables.

Nutritional Information:

- Calories: 400 | Fat: 30g | Carbs: 0g | Protein: 30g

TURKEY MEATBALLS

Prep: 15 mins | Cook: 20 mins | Serves: 4

Ingredients:

- US: 500g ground turkey, 1 egg, 50g breadcrumbs, 2 tablespoons grated Parmesan cheese, 1 garlic clove (minced), 1 tablespoon dried parsley, salt and pepper to taste, 30ml olive oil
- UK: 500g ground turkey, 1 egg, 50g breadcrumbs, 2 tablespoons grated Parmesan cheese, 1 garlic clove (minced), 1 tablespoon dried parsley, salt and pepper to taste, 30ml olive oil

Instructions:

1. Preheat your air fryer oven to 200°C (390°F).
2. In a large bowl, mix together turkey, egg, breadcrumbs, Parmesan, garlic, parsley, salt, and pepper.
3. Form the mixture into small meatballs (about 2 tablespoons each).
4. Lightly spray or brush the meatballs with olive oil.
5. Place the meatballs in the air fryer basket in a single layer.
6. Cook for 15-20 minutes, shaking the basket halfway through, until golden and cooked through.
7. Serve with marinara sauce and pasta.

Nutritional Information:

- Calories: 150 | Fat: 8g | Carbs: 5g | Protein: 15g

BUFFALO CHICKEN BITES

Prep: 10 mins | Cook: 15 mins | Serves: 4

Ingredients:

- US: 500g chicken breast (cut into bite-sized pieces), 60ml hot sauce, 2 tablespoons butter (melted), 1 teaspoon garlic powder, salt and pepper to taste, 30ml olive oil
- UK: 500g chicken breast (cut into bite-sized pieces), 60ml hot sauce, 2 tablespoons butter (melted), 1 teaspoon garlic powder, salt and pepper to taste, 30ml olive oil

Instructions:

1. Preheat your air fryer oven to 200°C (390°F).
2. In a bowl, mix hot sauce, melted butter, garlic powder, salt, and pepper.
3. Toss the chicken pieces in the hot sauce mixture.
4. Lightly spray or brush the chicken with olive oil.
5. Place the chicken bites in the air fryer basket in a single layer.
6. Cook for 10-15 minutes, shaking the basket halfway through, until the chicken is cooked and crispy.
7. Serve with blue cheese dressing and celery sticks.

Nutritional Information:

- Calories: 250 | Fat: 12g | Carbs: 5g | Protein:30g

CHICKEN SCHNITZEL

Prep: 15 mins | Cook: 15 mins | Serves: 4

Ingredients:

- US: 4 chicken breasts (pounded thin), 100g plain flour, 2 eggs (beaten), 100g breadcrumbs, 2 tablespoons Parmesan cheese (grated), salt and pepper to taste, 30ml olive oil
- UK: 4 chicken breasts (pounded thin), 100g plain flour, 2 eggs (beaten), 100g breadcrumbs, 2 tablespoons Parmesan cheese (grated), salt and pepper to taste, 30ml olive oil

Instructions:

1. Preheat your air fryer oven to 200°C (390°F).
2. Season the flour with salt and pepper.
3. Coat the chicken breasts in the seasoned flour, dip into the beaten eggs, and then coat with breadcrumbs mixed with Parmesan cheese.
4. Lightly spray or brush the chicken with olive oil.
5. Place the chicken schnitzels in the air fryer basket in a single layer.
6. Cook for 10-15 minutes, turning halfway through, until golden brown and crispy.
7. Serve with lemon wedges and a side salad.

Nutritional Information:

- Calories: 320 | Fat: 14g | Carbs: 25g | Protein: 25g

TANDOORI CHICKEN DRUMSTICKS

Prep: 10 mins | Cook: 25 mins | Serves: 4

Ingredients:

- US: 8 chicken drumsticks, 120g plain yogurt, 2 tablespoons lemon juice, 1 tablespoon ground cumin, 1 tablespoon ground coriander, 1 tablespoon ground turmeric, 1 tablespoon ground paprika, 1 teaspoon cayenne pepper, 2 garlic cloves (minced), salt to taste
- UK: 8 chicken drumsticks, 120g plain yogurt, 2 tablespoons lemon juice, 1 tablespoon ground cumin, 1 tablespoon ground coriander, 1 tablespoon ground turmeric, 1 tablespoon ground paprika, 1 teaspoon cayenne pepper, 2 garlic cloves (minced), salt to taste

Instructions:

1. Preheat your air fryer oven to 200°C (390°F).
2. In a bowl, mix together yogurt, lemon juice, cumin, coriander, turmeric, paprika, cayenne pepper, garlic, and salt.
3. Coat the chicken drumsticks in the yogurt mixture and marinate for at least 30 minutes.
4. Place the drumsticks in the air fryer basket in a single layer.
5. Cook for 20-25 minutes, turning halfway through, until the chicken is cooked through and slightly charred.
6. Serve with naan bread and a side of cucumber raita.

Nutritional Information:

- Calories: 260 | Fat: 15g | Carbs: 5g | Protein: 25g

MEATY MAINS

PERFECT PORK CHOPS

Prep: 10 mins | Cook: 15 mins | Serves: 4

Ingredients:

- US: 4 pork chops (about 200g each), 30ml olive oil, 2 teaspoons smoked paprika, 1 teaspoon garlic powder, salt, pepper
- UK: 4 pork chops (about 200g each), 30ml olive oil, 2 teaspoons smoked paprika, 1 teaspoon garlic powder, salt, pepper

Instructions:

1. Preheat your air fryer oven to 200°C (390°F) on the air fry setting.
2. Rub pork chops with olive oil, smoked paprika, garlic powder, salt, and pepper.
3. Place the pork chops in the air fryer basket in a single layer.
4. Air fry for 12-15 minutes, flipping halfway through, until the internal temperature reaches 63°C (145°F).
5. Let the pork chops rest for a few minutes before serving.
6. Serve hot with your favorite sides.

Nutritional Information:

- Calories: 300 | Fat: 15g | Carbs: 1g | Protein: 40g

BEEF MEATLOAF

Prep: 15 mins | Cook: 40 mins | Serves: 6

Ingredients:

- US: 500g ground beef, 1 onion (finely chopped), 1 egg, 60ml ketchup, 60ml breadcrumbs, 1 teaspoon garlic powder, salt, pepper
- UK: 500g ground beef, 1 onion (finely chopped), 1 egg, 60ml ketchup, 60ml breadcrumbs, 1 teaspoon garlic powder, salt, pepper

Instructions:

1. Preheat your air fryer oven to 180°C (350°F) on the bake setting.
2. In a bowl, mix together ground beef, onion, egg, ketchup, breadcrumbs, garlic powder, salt, and pepper.
3. Form the mixture into a loaf shape and place it on the air fryer rack.
4. Bake for 35-40 minutes, until the internal temperature reaches 71°C (160°F).
5. Let the meatloaf rest for 10 minutes before slicing.
6. Serve hot with mashed potatoes and vegetables.

Nutritional Information:

- Calories: 350 | Fat: 20g | Carbs: 10g | Protein: 30g

LAMB KOFTAS

Prep: 20 mins | Cook: 15 mins | Serves: 4

Ingredients:

- US: 500g ground lamb, 1 onion (finely chopped), 2 cloves garlic (minced), 1 teaspoon ground cumin, 1 teaspoon ground coriander, 1 teaspoon smoked paprika, salt, pepper
- UK: 500g ground lamb, 1 onion (finely chopped), 2 cloves garlic (minced), 1 teaspoon ground cumin, 1 teaspoon ground coriander, 1 teaspoon smoked paprika, salt, pepper

Instructions:

1. Preheat your air fryer oven to 200°C (390°F) on the air fry setting.
2. In a bowl, combine ground lamb, onion, garlic, cumin, coriander, paprika, salt, and pepper.
3. Divide the mixture into equal portions and shape them into oval koftas.
4. Place the koftas in the air fryer basket in a single layer.
5. Air fry for 12-15 minutes, turning halfway through, until browned and cooked through.
6. Serve hot with yogurt sauce and flatbread.

Nutritional Information:

- Calories: 400 | Fat: 30g | Carbs: 3g | Protein: 25g

STEAK WITH GARLIC BUTTER

Prep: 10 mins | Cook: 12 mins | Serves: 2

Ingredients:

- US: 2 steaks (about 250g each), 2 tablespoons butter (softened), 2 cloves garlic (minced), salt, pepper, chopped fresh parsley (for garnish)
- UK: 2 steaks (about 250g each), 2 tablespoons butter (softened), 2 cloves garlic (minced), salt, pepper, chopped fresh parsley (for garnish)

Instructions:

1. Preheat your air fryer oven to 200°C (390°F) on the air fry setting.
2. Season steaks generously with salt and pepper.
3. In a small bowl, mix together butter, minced garlic, salt, and pepper.
4. Spread the garlic butter mixture over both sides of the steaks.
5. Place the steaks in the air fryer basket.
6. Air fry for 10-12 minutes, flipping halfway through, for medium-rare doneness.
7. Let the steaks rest for a few minutes before slicing.
8. Garnish with chopped parsley and serve hot.

Nutritional Information:

- Calories: 450 | Fat: 25g | Carbs: 1g | Protein: 50g

BBQ RIBS

Prep: 20 mins | Cook: 40 mins | Serves: 4

Ingredients:

- US: 1 rack of pork ribs (about 1 kg), 240ml barbecue sauce, 2 teaspoons smoked paprika, 1 teaspoon garlic powder, salt, pepper
- UK: 1 rack of pork ribs (about 1 kg), 240ml barbecue sauce, 2 teaspoons smoked paprika, 1 teaspoon garlic powder, salt, pepper

Instructions:

1. Preheat your air fryer oven to 180°C (350°F) on the bake setting.
2. Rub ribs with smoked paprika, garlic powder, salt, and pepper.
3. Place the ribs on the air fryer rack, bone side down.
4. Bake for 30 minutes, then brush with barbecue sauce.
5. Bake for an additional 10 minutes, until the ribs are tender and caramelized.
6. Remove from the air fryer and let them rest for 5 minutes before slicing.
7. Serve hot with extra barbecue sauce on the side.

Nutritional Information:

- Calories: 600 | Fat: 35g | Carbs: 30g | Protein: 40g

SALISBURY STEAK

Prep: 20 mins | Cook: 25 mins | Serves: 4

Ingredients:

- US: 500g ground beef, 1 onion (finely chopped), 2 cloves garlic (minced), 240ml beef broth, 2 tablespoons Worcestershire sauce, 1 tablespoon tomato paste, 1 tablespoon cornstarch, salt, pepper, chopped fresh parsley
- UK: 500g ground beef, 1 onion (finely chopped), 2 cloves garlic (minced), 240ml beef broth, 2 tablespoons Worcestershire sauce, 1 tablespoon tomato paste, 1 tablespoon cornstarch, salt, pepper, chopped fresh parsley (for garnish)

Instructions:

1. Preheat your air fryer oven to 180°C (350°F) on the air fry setting.
2. In a bowl, mix together ground beef, onion, garlic, salt, and pepper.
3. Shape the mixture into oval patties.
4. Place the patties in the air fryer basket in a single layer.
5. Air fry for 12-15 minutes, flipping halfway through, until browned and cooked through.
6. In a small bowl, whisk together beef broth, Worcestershire sauce, tomato paste, and cornstarch.
7. Pour the sauce over the patties in the air fryer basket.
8. Air fry for an additional 5-7 minutes, until the sauce thickens.
9. Garnish with chopped parsley before serving.
10. Serve hot with mashed potatoes or rice.

Nutritional Information:

- Calories: 350 | Fat: 20g | Carbs: 10g | Protein: 30g

ITALIAN MEATBALLS

Prep: 20 mins | Cook: 20 mins | Serves: 4

Ingredients:

- US: 500g ground beef, 1 onion (finely chopped), 2 cloves garlic (minced), 50g breadcrumbs, 1 egg, 1 teaspoon dried oregano, 1 teaspoon dried basil, salt, pepper
- UK: 500g ground beef, 1 onion (finely chopped), 2 cloves garlic (minced), 50g breadcrumbs, 1 egg, 1 teaspoon dried oregano, 1 teaspoon dried basil, salt, pepper

Instructions:

1. Preheat your air fryer oven to 180°C (350°F) on the air fry setting.
2. In a bowl, mix together ground beef, onion, garlic, breadcrumbs, egg, oregano, basil, salt, and pepper.
3. Shape the mixture into meatballs of equal size.
4. Place the meatballs in the air fryer basket in a single layer.
5. Air fry for 15-20 minutes, shaking halfway through, until browned and cooked through.
6. Serve hot with marinara sauce and spaghetti.

Nutritional Information:

- Calories: 350 | Fat: 20g | Carbs: 10g | Protein: 30g

HONEY GLAZED HAM

Prep: 15 mins | Cook: 30 mins | Serves: 6

Ingredients:

- US: 1 kg boneless ham, 60ml honey, 30ml Dijon mustard, 1 tablespoon brown sugar, 1 teaspoon ground cloves
- UK: 1 kg boneless ham, 60ml honey, 30ml Dijon mustard, 1 tablespoon brown sugar, 1 teaspoon ground cloves

Instructions:

1. Preheat your air fryer oven to 160°C (320°F) on the bake setting.
2. Score the surface of the ham in a diamond pattern.
3. In a bowl, mix together honey, Dijon mustard, brown sugar, and ground cloves.
4. Brush the honey mixture over the ham, ensuring it's evenly coated.
5. Place the ham on the air fryer rack.
6. Bake for 25-30 minutes, brushing with more glaze halfway through, until heated through and caramelized.
7. Remove from the air fryer and let it rest for 10 minutes before slicing.
8. Serve warm as a main dish or slice for sandwiches.

Nutritional Information:

- Calories: 250 | Fat: 10g | Carbs: 15g | Protein: 25g

BEEF JERKY

Prep: 20 mins | Cook: 4 hours | Serves: 8

Ingredients:

- US: 500g beef sirloin or flank steak (sliced thinly), 120ml soy sauce, 2 tablespoons Worcestershire sauce, 1 tablespoon brown sugar, 1 teaspoon smoked paprika, 1 teaspoon garlic powder, 1/2 teaspoon black pepper
- UK: 500g beef sirloin or flank steak (sliced thinly), 120ml soy sauce, 2 tablespoons Worcestershire sauce, 1 tablespoon brown sugar, 1 teaspoon smoked paprika, 1 teaspoon garlic powder, 1/2 teaspoon black pepper

Instructions:

1. Preheat your air fryer oven to 70°C (160°F) on the dehydrate setting.
2. In a bowl, combine soy sauce, Worcestershire sauce, brown sugar, smoked paprika, garlic powder, and black pepper.
3. Add the beef slices to the marinade and toss to coat evenly.
4. Place the beef slices on the air fryer racks in a single layer, leaving space between each slice.
5. Dehydrate for 3-4 hours, depending on desired chewiness, flipping halfway through.
6. Remove from the air fryer and let the beef jerky cool completely before storing in an airtight container.

Nutritional Information:

- Calories: 150 | Fat: 5g | Carbs: 3g | Protein: 25g

STUFFED PORK TENDERLOIN

Prep: 30 mins | Cook: 30 mins | Serves: 4

Ingredients:

- US: 500g pork tenderloin, 100g spinach (chopped), 100g feta cheese (crumbled), 2 cloves garlic (minced), 1 teaspoon dried thyme, salt, pepper, olive oil
- UK: 500g pork tenderloin, 100g spinach (chopped), 100g feta cheese (crumbled), 2 cloves garlic (minced), 1 teaspoon dried thyme, salt, pepper, olive oil

Instructions:

1. Preheat your air fryer oven to 180°C (350°F) on the air fry setting.
2. Butterfly the pork tenderloin by slicing it horizontally, but not all the way through.
3. Open the pork tenderloin and pound it to an even thickness.
4. Season the inside with salt, pepper, and dried thyme.
5. Layer spinach, garlic, and feta cheese on one side of the pork.
6. Fold the pork over the filling and secure with kitchen twine.
7. Rub olive oil, salt, and pepper over the pork.
8. Place the stuffed pork tenderloin in the air fryer basket.
9. Air fry for 25-30 minutes, turning halfway through, until the internal temperature reaches 63°C (145°F).
10. Let it rest for 5 minutes before slicing.
11. Serve hot with roasted vegetables.

Nutritional Information:

- Calories: 300 | Fat: 15g | Carbs: 5g | Protein: 35g

CRISPY FISH AND CHIPS

Prep: 15 mins | Cook: 20 mins | Serves: 4

Ingredients:

- US: 4 cod fillets (about 150g each), 200g potato (cut into fries), 2 tablespoons olive oil, salt, pepper
- UK: 4 cod fillets (about 150g each), 200g potato (cut into chips), 2 tablespoons olive oil, salt, pepper

Instructions:

1. Preheat your air fryer oven to 200°C (390°F).
2. Prepare the fries by tossing potato sticks with olive oil, salt, and pepper.
3. Place the fries in a single layer in the air fryer basket.
4. Cook for 15-20 minutes, shaking halfway through, until golden and crispy.
5. Season cod fillets with salt and pepper.
6. Arrange the fillets in the air fryer basket, ensuring they aren't overlapping.
7. Air fry for 10-12 minutes, until the fish is cooked through and the coating is crispy.
8. Serve hot with the crispy fries.

Nutritional Information:

- Calories: 350 | Fat: 12g | Carbs: 30g | Protein: 28g

LEMON GARLIC SALMON

Prep: 10 mins | Cook: 12 mins | Serves: 4

Ingredients:

- US: 4 salmon fillets (about 150g each), 60ml olive oil, 2 cloves garlic (minced), 1 lemon (juiced and zested), salt, pepper, chopped fresh parsley
- UK: 4 salmon fillets (about 150g each), 60ml olive oil, 2 cloves garlic (minced), 1 lemon (juiced and zested), salt, pepper, chopped fresh parsley

Instructions:

1. Preheat your air fryer oven to 180°C (350°F).
2. In a bowl, combine olive oil, minced garlic, lemon juice, lemon zest, salt, and pepper.
3. Brush the mixture over the salmon fillets.
4. Place the fillets in the air fryer basket.
5. Air fry for 10-12 minutes, depending on thickness, until salmon is cooked through.
6. Sprinkle with fresh parsley before serving.

Nutritional Information:

- Calories: 300 | Fat: 18g | Carbs: 2g | Protein: 30g

COCONUT SHRIMP

Prep: 20 mins | Cook: 10 mins | Serves: 4

Ingredients:

- US: 500g large shrimp (peeled and deveined), 100g breadcrumbs, 100g shredded coconut, 2 eggs (beaten), salt, pepper, sweet chili sauce (for dipping)
- UK: 500g large prawns (peeled and deveined), 100g breadcrumbs, 100g shredded coconut, 2 eggs (beaten), salt, pepper, sweet chili sauce (for dipping)

Instructions:

1. Preheat your air fryer oven to 200°C (390°F).
2. In separate bowls, place breadcrumbs and shredded coconut.
3. Season shrimp with salt and pepper.
4. Dip each shrimp in beaten eggs, then coat with breadcrumb-coconut mixture.
5. Arrange shrimp in a single layer in the air fryer basket.
6. Air fry for 8-10 minutes, flipping halfway, until golden and crispy.
7. Serve hot with sweet chili sauce.

Nutritional Information:

- Calories: 280 | Fat: 12g | Carbs: 20g | Protein: 22g

CAJUN TILAPIA

Prep: 10 mins | Cook: 12 mins | Serves: 4

Ingredients:

- US: 4 tilapia fillets (about 150g each), 30ml olive oil, 2 teaspoons Cajun seasoning, 1 teaspoon paprika, salt, pepper, lemon wedges (for serving)
- UK: 4 tilapia fillets (about 150g each), 30ml olive oil, 2 teaspoons Cajun seasoning, 1 teaspoon paprika, salt, pepper, lemon wedges (for serving)

Instructions:

1. Preheat your air fryer oven to 180°C (350°F).
2. Brush tilapia fillets with olive oil.
3. Season both sides with Cajun seasoning, paprika, salt, and pepper.
4. Place the fillets in the air fryer basket.
5. Air fry for 10-12 minutes, until fish flakes easily with a fork.
6. Serve hot with lemon wedges.

Nutritional Information:

- Calories: 200 | Fat: 10g | Carbs: 2g | Protein: 26g

CRAB CAKES

Prep: 20 mins | Cook: 15 mins | Serves: 4

Ingredients:

- US: 250g crabmeat, 1 egg, 2 tablespoons mayonnaise, 1 tablespoon Dijon mustard, 1 teaspoon Old Bay seasoning, 50g breadcrumbs, olive oil (for brushing)
- UK: 250g crabmeat, 1 egg, 2 tablespoons mayonnaise, 1 tablespoon Dijon mustard, 1 teaspoon Old Bay seasoning, 50g breadcrumbs, olive oil (for brushing)

Instructions:

1. Preheat your air fryer oven to 200°C (390°F).
2. In a bowl, combine crabmeat, egg, mayonnaise, Dijon mustard, Old Bay seasoning, and breadcrumbs.
3. Form mixture into patties.
4. Brush patties with olive oil.
5. Place crab cakes in the air fryer basket.
6. Air fry for 12-15 minutes, flipping halfway, until golden brown and heated through.
7. Serve hot with tartar sauce.

Nutritional Information:

- Calories: 220 | Fat: 12g | Carbs: 10g | Protein: 18g

GARLIC BUTTER SCALLOPS

Prep: 10 mins | Cook: 8 mins | Serves: 4

Ingredients:

- US: 500g scallops, 60g butter (melted), 3 cloves garlic (minced), salt, pepper, chopped fresh parsley
- UK: 500g scallops, 60g butter (melted), 3 cloves garlic (minced), salt, pepper, chopped fresh parsley

Instructions:

1. Preheat your air fryer oven to 200°C (390°F).
2. In a bowl, mix melted butter, minced garlic, salt, and pepper.
3. Add scallops to the bowl and toss to coat.
4. Place scallops in the air fryer basket.
5. Air fry for 6-8 minutes, shaking halfway, until scallops are opaque and cooked through.
6. Sprinkle with chopped parsley before serving.

Nutritional Information:

- Calories: 250 | Fat: 10g | Carbs: 5g | Protein: 35g

TERIYAKI SALMON

Prep: 15 mins | Cook: 12 mins | Serves: 4

Ingredients:

- US: 4 salmon fillets (about 150g each), 120ml teriyaki sauce, 30ml soy sauce, 1 tablespoon honey, sesame seeds (for garnish)
- UK: 4 salmon fillets (about 150g each), 120ml teriyaki sauce, 30ml soy sauce, 1 tablespoon honey, sesame seeds (for garnish)

Instructions:

1. Preheat your air fryer oven to 180°C (350°F).
2. In a bowl, whisk together teriyaki sauce, soy sauce, and honey.
3. Marinate salmon fillets in the mixture for 10 minutes.
4. Place salmon fillets in the air fryer basket, reserving marinade.
5. Air fry for 10-12 minutes, basting with reserved marinade halfway through, until salmon is cooked through.
6. Sprinkle with sesame seeds before serving.

Nutritional Information:

- Calories: 300 | Fat: 12g | Carbs: 15g | Protein: 30g

FISH FINGERS

Prep: 15 mins | Cook: 10 mins | Serves: 4

Ingredients:

- US: 500g white fish fillets (cut into strips), 100g breadcrumbs, 2 eggs (beaten), salt, pepper, lemon wedges (for serving)
- UK: 500g white fish fillets (cut into strips), 100g breadcrumbs, 2 eggs (beaten), salt, pepper, lemon wedges (for serving)

Instructions:

1. Preheat your air fryer oven to 200°C (390°F).
2. Season fish strips with salt and pepper.
3. Dip each strip in beaten eggs, then coat with breadcrumbs.
4. Arrange fish fingers in a single layer in the air fryer basket.
5. Air fry for 8-10 minutes, flipping halfway through, until golden and crispy.
6. Serve hot with lemon wedges and tartar sauce.

Nutritional Information:

- Calories: 280 | Fat: 10g | Carbs: 20g | Protein: 25g

LEMON PEPPER COD

Prep: 10 mins | Cook: 12 mins | Serves: 4

Ingredients:

- US: 4 cod fillets (about 150g each), 60ml olive oil, 1 lemon (juiced and zested), 2 teaspoons black pepper, salt, chopped fresh dill (for garnish)
- UK: 4 cod fillets (about 150g each), 60ml olive oil, 1 lemon (juiced and zested), 2 teaspoons black pepper, salt, chopped fresh dill (for garnish)

Instructions:

1. Preheat your air fryer oven to 180°C (350°F).
2. In a bowl, whisk together olive oil, lemon juice, lemon zest, black pepper, and salt.
3. Brush the mixture over the cod fillets.
4. Place the fillets in the air fryer basket.
5. Air fry for 10-12 minutes, until fish flakes easily with a fork.
6. Garnish with chopped fresh dill before serving.

Nutritional Information:

- Calories: 250 | Fat: 12g | Carbs: 2g | Protein: 28g

CRISPY CALAMARI RINGS

Prep: 20 mins | Cook: 10 mins | Serves: 4

Ingredients:

- US: 400g calamari rings (thawed if frozen), 100g breadcrumbs, 50g cornmeal, 1 teaspoon paprika, salt, pepper, lemon wedges (for serving)
- UK: 400g calamari rings (thawed if frozen), 100g breadcrumbs, 50g cornmeal, 1 teaspoon paprika, salt, pepper, lemon wedges (for serving)

Instructions:

1. Preheat your air fryer oven to 200°C (390°F).
2. In a bowl, mix breadcrumbs, cornmeal, paprika, salt, and pepper.
3. Coat calamari rings in the breadcrumb mixture.
4. Arrange calamari rings in a single layer in the air fryer basket.
5. Air fry for 8-10 minutes, shaking halfway, until golden and crispy.
6. Serve hot with lemon wedges and tartar sauce.

Nutritional Information:

- Calories: 220 | Fat: 8g | Carbs: 20g | Protein: 18g

VEGETARIAN AND VEGAN DELIGHTS

CRISPY TOFU CUBES

Prep: 15 mins | Cook: 20 mins | Serves: 4

Ingredients:

- US: 400g firm tofu, 2 tablespoons soy sauce, 1 tablespoon cornstarch, 1 teaspoon garlic powder, 1 teaspoon smoked paprika, salt and pepper
- UK: 400g firm tofu, 2 tablespoons soy sauce, 1 tablespoon cornstarch, 1 teaspoon garlic powder, 1 teaspoon smoked paprika, salt and pepper

Instructions:

1. Preheat your air fryer oven to 200°C (390°F).
2. Press tofu to remove excess water, then cut into cubes.
3. In a bowl, combine tofu cubes with soy sauce, cornstarch, garlic powder, smoked paprika, salt, and pepper until evenly coated.
4. Arrange tofu cubes in a single layer in the air fryer basket.
5. Cook for 15-20 minutes, shaking halfway through, until tofu is crispy and golden brown.
6. Serve hot as a snack or with your favorite dipping sauce.

Nutritional Information:

- Calories: 180 | Fat: 8g | Carbs: 8g | Protein: 18g

STUFFED PORTOBELLO MUSHROOMS

Prep: 20 mins | Cook: 15 mins | Serves: 4

Ingredients:

- US: 4 large portobello mushrooms, 1 cup spinach (chopped), 1/2 cup sun-dried tomatoes (chopped), 1/2 cup feta cheese (crumbled), 2 cloves garlic (minced), salt and pepper, 30ml olive oil
- UK: 4 large portobello mushrooms, 1 cup spinach (chopped), 1/2 cup sun-dried tomatoes (chopped), 1/2 cup feta cheese (crumbled), 2 cloves garlic (minced), salt and pepper, 30ml olive oil

Instructions:

1. Preheat your air fryer oven to 180°C (350°F).
2. Remove stems from mushrooms and gently scrape out gills.
3. In a bowl, combine spinach, sun-dried tomatoes, feta cheese, garlic, salt, and pepper.
4. Stuff each mushroom cap with filling mixture.
5. Brush mushrooms with olive oil.
6. Place mushrooms in the air fryer basket in a single layer.
7. Cook for 12-15 minutes, until mushrooms are tender and filling is heated through.
8. Serve hot as a flavorful appetizer or main dish.

Nutritional Information:

- Calories: 150 | Fat: 8g | Carbs: 10g | Protein: 6g

FALAFEL

Prep: 20 mins | Cook: 15 mins | Serves: 4

Ingredients:

- US: 400g canned chickpeas (drained and rinsed), 1 small onion (chopped), 2 cloves garlic (minced), 2 tablespoons chopped fresh parsley, 1 teaspoon ground cumin, 1 teaspoon ground coriander, 1/2 teaspoon salt, 1/4 teaspoon black pepper, 30ml olive oil
- UK: 400g canned chickpeas (drained and rinsed), 1 small onion (chopped), 2 cloves garlic (minced), 2 tablespoons chopped fresh parsley, 1 teaspoon ground cumin, 1 teaspoon ground coriander, 1/2 teaspoon salt, 1/4 teaspoon black pepper, 30ml olive oil

Instructions:

1. Preheat your air fryer oven to 200°C (390°F).
2. Combine chickpeas, onion, garlic, parsley, cumin, coriander, salt, and pepper in a food processor. Pulse until mixture is coarse but well combined.
3. Shape mixture into small balls or patties.
4. Brush falafel with olive oil.
5. Place falafel in the air fryer basket in a single layer.
6. Cook for 12-15 minutes, flipping halfway through, until falafel is crispy and browned.
7. Serve hot with tahini sauce, salad, or in pita bread.

Nutritional Information:

- Calories: 220 | Fat: 10g | Carbs: 25g | Protein: 10g

CRISPY CHICKPEAS

Prep: 5 mins | Cook: 20 mins | Serves: 4

Ingredients:

- US: 400g canned chickpeas (drained and rinsed), 2 tablespoons olive oil, 1 teaspoon smoked paprika, 1/2 teaspoon cumin, 1/2 teaspoon garlic powder, salt and pepper
- UK: 400g canned chickpeas (drained and rinsed), 2 tablespoons olive oil, 1 teaspoon smoked paprika, 1/2 teaspoon cumin, 1/2 teaspoon garlic powder, salt and pepper

Instructions:

1. Preheat your air fryer oven to 200°C (390°F).
2. Pat dry chickpeas with paper towels to remove excess moisture.
3. In a bowl, toss chickpeas with olive oil, smoked paprika, cumin, garlic powder, salt, and pepper until well coated.
4. Spread chickpeas in a single layer in the air fryer basket.
5. Cook for 15-20 minutes, shaking halfway through, until chickpeas are crispy.
6. Sprinkle with additional salt if desired.
7. Serve hot as a crunchy snack or salad topper.

Nutritional Information:

- Calories: 180 | Fat: 7g | Carbs: 20g | Protein: 8g

VEGETABLE SPRING ROLLS

Prep: 30 mins | Cook: 15 mins | Serves: 4

Ingredients:

- US: 8 spring roll wrappers, 100g vermicelli noodles (cooked), 1 cup shredded cabbage, 1 carrot (julienned), 1/2 red bell pepper (julienned), 1/2 cucumber (julienned), 2 tablespoons soy sauce, 1 tablespoon sesame oil
- UK: 8 spring roll wrappers, 100g vermicelli noodles (cooked), 1 cup shredded cabbage, 1 carrot (julienned), 1/2 red bell pepper (julienned), 1/2 cucumber (julienned), 2 tablespoons soy sauce, 1 tablespoon sesame oil

Instructions:

1. Preheat your air fryer oven to 180°C (350°F).
2. Prepare vermicelli noodles according to package instructions and let cool.
3. Combine shredded cabbage, carrot, bell pepper, cucumber, soy sauce, and sesame oil in a bowl.
4. Soak spring roll wrappers in warm water until pliable.
5. Place a portion of vegetable mixture and noodles on each wrapper, then fold sides over and roll tightly.
6. Brush spring rolls with oil.
7. Arrange spring rolls in the air fryer basket in a single layer.
8. Cook for 12-15 minutes, until golden and crispy.
9. Serve hot with dipping sauce.

Nutritional Information:

- Calories: 180 | Fat: 2g | Carbs: 35g | Protein: 5g

CAULIFLOWER "WINGS"

Prep: 15 mins | Cook: 25 mins | Serves: 4

Ingredients:

- US: 1 medium cauliflower (cut into florets), 1 cup breadcrumbs, 1 teaspoon garlic powder, 1 teaspoon paprika, 1/2 teaspoon salt, 1/4 teaspoon black pepper, 1/2 cup buffalo sauce, 30ml melted butter or olive oil
- UK: 1 medium cauliflower (cut into florets), 1 cup breadcrumbs, 1 teaspoon garlic powder, 1 teaspoon paprika, 1/2 teaspoon salt, 1/4 teaspoon black pepper, 1/2 cup buffalo sauce, 30ml melted butter or olive oil

Instructions:

1. Preheat your air fryer oven to 200°C (390°F).
2. In a bowl, combine breadcrumbs, garlic powder, paprika, salt, and pepper.
3. Dip cauliflower florets in melted butter or olive oil, then coat with breadcrumb mixture.
4. Arrange coated cauliflower florets in the air fryer basket in a single layer.
5. Cook for 20-25 minutes, shaking halfway through, until cauliflower is crispy and golden.
6. Toss cooked cauliflower in buffalo sauce until well coated.
7. Serve hot with celery sticks and ranch dressing.

Nutritional Information:

- Calories: 180 | Fat: 8g | Carbs: 20g | Protein: 5g

EGGPLANT PARMESAN

Prep: 30 mins | Cook: 20 mins | Serves: 4

Ingredients:

- US: 1 large eggplant (sliced into rounds), 1 cup breadcrumbs, 1/2 cup grated Parmesan cheese, 2 eggs (beaten), 1 cup marinara sauce, 1 cup shredded mozzarella cheese, fresh basil leaves (for garnish), salt and pepper
- UK: 1 large eggplant (sliced into rounds), 1 cup breadcrumbs, 1/2 cup grated Parmesan cheese, 2 eggs (beaten), 1 cup marinara sauce, 1 cup shredded mozzarella cheese, fresh basil leaves (for garnish), salt and pepper

Instructions:

1. Preheat your air fryer oven to 180°C (350°F).
2. Dip eggplant slices into beaten eggs, then coat with breadcrumbs mixed with Parmesan cheese.
3. Arrange coated eggplant slices in the air fryer basket in a single layer.
4. Cook for 10-12 minutes, flipping halfway through, until eggplant is golden and crispy.
5. Layer cooked eggplant slices with marinara sauce and mozzarella cheese.
6. Return to air fryer and cook for another 5-7 minutes, until cheese is melted and bubbly.
7. Garnish with fresh basil leaves before serving.

Nutritional Information:

- Calories: 250 | Fat: 10g | Carbs: 30g | Protein: 12g

VEGAN "MEATBALLS"

Prep: 30 mins | Cook: 20 mins | Serves: 4

Ingredients:

- US: 400g cooked lentils, 1 cup breadcrumbs, 1/4 cup ground flaxseed, 1/4 cup nutritional yeast, 1 tablespoon soy sauce, 1 teaspoon dried oregano, 1/2 teaspoon garlic powder, 1/2 teaspoon onion powder, salt and pepper, 30ml olive oil
- UK: 400g cooked lentils, 1 cup breadcrumbs, 1/4 cup ground flaxseed, 1/4 cup nutritional yeast, 1 tablespoon soy sauce, 1 teaspoon dried oregano, 1/2 teaspoon garlic powder, 1/2 teaspoon onion powder, salt and pepper, 30ml olive oil

Instructions:

1. Preheat your air fryer oven to 180°C (350°F).
2. In a food processor, pulse cooked lentils until partially mashed.
3. Transfer lentils to a bowl and add breadcrumbs, ground flaxseed, nutritional yeast, soy sauce, oregano, garlic powder, onion powder, salt, and pepper. Mix until well combined.
4. Shape mixture into small balls.
5. Brush balls with olive oil.
6. Arrange balls in the air fryer basket in a single layer.
7. Cook for 15-20 minutes, shaking halfway through, until meatballs are crispy and cooked through.
8. Serve hot with marinara sauce or atop pasta.

Nutritional Information:

- Calories: 220 | Fat: 8g | Carbs: 30g | Protein: 10g

VEGETABLE PAKORAS

Prep: 20 mins | Cook: 15 mins | Serves: 4

Ingredients:

- US: 1 cup chickpea flour, 1/2 cup water, 1/2 teaspoon ground cumin, 1/2 teaspoon ground coriander, 1/2 teaspoon turmeric powder, 1/4 teaspoon baking powder, salt and pepper, 1 cup mixed vegetables (such as cauliflower florets, sliced onions, and spinach leaves), 30ml vegetable oil (for brushing)
- UK: 1 cup chickpea flour, 1/2 cup water, 1/2 teaspoon ground cumin, 1/2 teaspoon ground coriander, 1/2 teaspoon turmeric powder, 1/4 teaspoon baking powder, salt and pepper, 1 cup mixed vegetables (such as cauliflower florets, sliced onions, and spinach leaves), 30ml vegetable oil (for brushing)

Instructions:

1. Preheat your air fryer oven to 180°C (350°F).
2. Whisk together chickpea flour, water, cumin, coriander, turmeric powder, baking powder, salt, and pepper.
3. Stir in mixed vegetables until well coated.
4. Scoop tablespoonfuls of batter and vegetables onto air fryer basket, flattening slightly.
5. Brush tops with vegetable oil.
6. Cook for 12-15 minutes, flipping halfway through, until pakoras are golden and crispy.
7. Serve hot with chutney or yogurt sauce.

Nutritional Information:

- Calories: 160 | Fat: 5g | Carbs: 25g | Protein: 6g

ZUCCHINI FRITTERS

Prep: 20 mins | Cook: 15 mins | Serves: 4

Ingredients:

- US: 2 medium zucchinis (grated), 1/2 cup breadcrumbs, 1/4 cup grated Parmesan cheese, 1 egg (beaten), 1/4 teaspoon garlic powder, 1/4 teaspoon onion powder, salt and pepper, 30ml olive oil
- UK: 2 medium zucchinis (grated), 1/2 cup breadcrumbs, 1/4 cup grated Parmesan cheese, 1 egg (beaten), 1/4 teaspoon garlic powder, 1/4 teaspoon onion powder, salt and pepper, 30ml olive oil

Instructions:

1. Preheat your air fryer oven to 180°C (350°F).
2. Place grated zucchini in a clean kitchen towel and squeeze out excess moisture.
3. In a bowl, combine zucchini, breadcrumbs, Parmesan cheese, egg, garlic powder, onion powder, salt, and pepper until mixture holds together.
4. Form mixture into small patties.
5. Brush both sides of patties with olive oil.
6. Arrange patties in the air fryer basket in a single layer.
7. Cook for 12-15 minutes, flipping halfway through, until fritters are golden and crispy.
8. Serve hot with sour cream or yogurt sauce.

Nutritional Information:

- Calories: 160 | Fat: 7g | Carbs: 20g | Protein: 6g

CHOCOLATE CHIP COOKIES

Prep: 15 mins | Cook: 10 mins | Serves: 12 cookies

Ingredients:

- US: 200g all-purpose flour, 1/2 teaspoon baking soda, 1/2 teaspoon salt, 115g unsalted butter (softened), 100g granulated sugar, 100g brown sugar, 1 large egg, 1 teaspoon vanilla extract, 150g chocolate chips
- UK: 200g plain flour, 1/2 teaspoon baking soda, 1/2 teaspoon salt, 115g unsalted butter (softened), 100g caster sugar, 100g soft light brown sugar, 1 large egg, 1 teaspoon vanilla extract, 150g chocolate chips

Instructions:

1. Preheat your air fryer oven to 180°C (350°F).
2. In a bowl, whisk together flour, baking soda, and salt.
3. In another bowl, beat butter, granulated sugar, and brown sugar until creamy.
4. Add egg and vanilla extract to the butter mixture and beat until combined.
5. Gradually add the flour mixture to the wet ingredients, mixing until just combined.
6. Fold in chocolate chips.
7. Drop tablespoon-sized balls of dough onto a parchment-lined air fryer basket, leaving space between each cookie.
8. Cook for 8-10 minutes until edges are golden brown.
9. Remove and let cool on a wire rack before serving.

Nutritional Information:

- Calories: 250 | Fat: 12g | Carbs: 34g | Protein: 3g

APPLE TURNOVERS

Prep: 20 mins | Cook: 15 mins | Serves: 4 turnovers

Ingredients:

- US: 2 apples (peeled, cored, and diced), 1 tablespoon lemon juice, 2 tablespoons granulated sugar, 1/2 teaspoon ground cinnamon, 1 sheet puff pastry (thawed), 1 egg (beaten), 1 tablespoon powdered sugar (for dusting)
- UK: 2 apples (peeled, cored, and diced), 1 tablespoon lemon juice, 2 tablespoons caster sugar, 1/2 teaspoon ground cinnamon, 1 sheet puff pastry (thawed), 1 egg (beaten), 1 tablespoon icing sugar (for dusting)

Instructions:

1. Preheat your air fryer oven to 180°C (350°F).
2. In a bowl, toss diced apples with lemon juice, sugar, and cinnamon.
3. Roll out puff pastry and cut into 4 squares.
4. Divide apple mixture evenly among the squares.
5. Fold each square into a triangle and crimp the edges with a fork to seal.
6. Brush turnovers with beaten egg.
7. Place turnovers in the air fryer basket and cook for 12-15 minutes until golden brown.
8. Remove from air fryer and let cool slightly before dusting with powdered sugar.
9. Serve warm.

Nutritional Information:

- Calories: 280 | Fat: 14g | Carbs: 36g | Protein: 3g

Prep: 15 mins | Cook: 50 mins | Serves: 1 loaf

Ingredients:

- US: 3 ripe bananas, 100g granulated sugar, 1 egg, 75g unsalted butter (melted), 1 teaspoon vanilla extract, 190g all-purpose flour, 1 teaspoon baking powder, 1/2 teaspoon baking soda, 1/2 teaspoon salt, 1/2 teaspoon ground cinnamon
- UK: 3 ripe bananas, 100g caster sugar, 1 egg, 75g unsalted butter (melted), 1 teaspoon vanilla extract, 190g plain flour, 1 teaspoon baking powder, 1/2 teaspoon baking soda, 1/2 teaspoon salt, 1/2 teaspoon ground cinnamon

Instructions:

1. Preheat your air fryer oven to 160°C (320°F).
2. In a bowl, mash bananas with sugar, egg, melted butter, and vanilla extract.
3. In another bowl, whisk together flour, baking powder, baking soda, salt, and cinnamon.
4. Fold dry ingredients into wet ingredients until just combined.
5. Pour batter into a greased loaf pan that fits in your air fryer oven.
6. Place loaf pan in the air fryer basket.
7. Cook for 45-50 minutes until a toothpick inserted into the center comes out clean.
8. Remove from air fryer and let cool in the pan for 10 minutes before transferring to a wire rack to cool completely.
9. Slice and serve.

Nutritional Information:

- Calories: 220 | Fat: 7g | Carbs: 36g | Protein: 3g

Prep: 20 mins | Cook: 10 mins | Serves: 12 doughnuts

Ingredients:

- US: 250ml milk, 50g granulated sugar, 7g active dry yeast, 60g unsalted butter (melted), 1 egg, 1 teaspoon vanilla extract, 350g all-purpose flour, 1/2 teaspoon salt, oil spray (for frying), 100g granulated sugar (for coating), 1 tablespoon ground cinnamon
- UK: 250ml milk, 50g caster sugar, 7g active dry yeast, 60g unsalted butter (melted), 1 egg, 1 teaspoon vanilla extract, 350g plain flour, 1/2 teaspoon salt, oil spray (for frying), 100g caster sugar (for coating), 1 tablespoon ground cinnamon

Instructions:

1. Heat milk until warm but not hot, about 45°C (110°F).
2. Stir in sugar and yeast. Let sit for 5 minutes until foamy.
3. Mix in melted butter, egg, and vanilla extract.
4. In a separate bowl, combine flour and salt. Gradually add to wet ingredients, stirring until dough forms.
5. Knead dough on a floured surface until smooth and elastic, about 5 minutes.
6. Cover and let rise in a warm place for 1 hour or until doubled in size.
7. Punch down dough and roll out to 1cm thickness.
8. Use a doughnut cutter or a round cutter and a smaller cutter for the center to cut out doughnuts.
9. Place doughnuts on a parchment-lined air fryer basket, leaving space between each one.
10. Cook at 180°C (350°F) for 5 minutes. Flip doughnuts and cook for an additional 3-5 minutes until golden brown.
11. Remove from air fryer and immediately roll in cinnamon sugar mixture.
12. Serve warm.

Nutritional Information:

- Calories: 180 | Fat: 6g | Carbs: 28g | Protein: 3g

Prep: 15 mins | Cook: 20 mins | Serves: 12 muffins

Ingredients:

- US: 250g all-purpose flour, 150g granulated sugar, 2 teaspoons baking powder, 1/2 teaspoon baking soda, 1/2 teaspoon salt, 120ml milk, 120ml vegetable oil, 2 eggs, 1 teaspoon vanilla extract, 200g fresh or frozen blueberries
- UK: 250g plain flour, 150g caster sugar, 2 teaspoons baking powder, 1/2 teaspoon baking soda, 1/2 teaspoon salt, 120ml milk, 120ml vegetable oil, 2 eggs, 1 teaspoon vanilla extract, 200g fresh or frozen blueberries

Instructions:

1. Preheat your air fryer oven to 180°C (350°F).
2. In a bowl, whisk together flour, sugar, baking powder, baking soda, and salt.
3. In another bowl, whisk together milk, vegetable oil, eggs, and vanilla extract.
4. Pour wet ingredients into dry ingredients and mix until just combined.
5. Gently fold in blueberries.
6. Line muffin tin with paper liners or grease well.
7. Spoon batter into muffin cups, filling each about two-thirds full.
8. Place muffin tin in the air fryer basket.
9. Cook for 18-22 minutes until a toothpick inserted into the center comes out clean.
10. Remove from air fryer and let cool in the tin for 5 minutes before transferring to a wire rack to cool completely.
11. Serve warm or at room temperature.

Nutritional Information:

- Calories: 200 | Fat: 9g | Carbs: 28g | Protein: 3g

CHURROS

Prep: 20 mins | Cook: 15 mins | Serves: 12 churros

Ingredients:

- US: 250ml water, 2 tablespoons granulated sugar, 1/2 teaspoon salt, 120g unsalted butter, 250g all-purpose flour,
- 2 eggs, 1/2 teaspoon vanilla extract, oil spray (for frying), 100g granulated sugar, 1 tablespoon ground cinnamon
- UK: 250ml water, 2 tablespoons caster sugar, 1/2 teaspoon salt, 120g unsalted butter, 250g plain flour, 2 eggs, 1/2 teaspoon vanilla extract, oil spray (for frying), 100g caster sugar, 1 tablespoon ground cinnamon

Instructions:

1. In a saucepan, combine water, sugar, salt, and butter. Bring to a boil over medium heat.
2. Remove from heat and stir in flour until mixture forms a ball.
3. Let cool for 5 minutes, then beat in eggs one at a time until smooth.
4. Stir in vanilla extract.
5. Transfer dough to a piping bag fitted with a large star tip.
6. Pipe dough into 5-inch strips onto a parchment-lined air fryer basket.
7. Spray churros lightly with oil spray.
8. Cook at 180°C (350°F) for 8 minutes. Flip churros and cook for an additional 5-7 minutes until golden brown and crisp.
9. Remove from air fryer and immediately roll in cinnamon sugar mixture.
10. Serve warm with chocolate sauce or dulce de leche.

Nutritional Information:

- Calories: 180 | Fat: 7g | Carbs: 28g | Protein: 3g

Prep: 15 mins | Cook: 10 mins | Serves: 1 pizza

Ingredients:

- US: 1 small pizza dough ball (store-bought or homemade), 4 tablespoons marinara sauce, 50g mozzarella cheese (shredded), 50g pepperoni slices, 1/4 teaspoon dried oregano, 1/4 teaspoon dried basil, olive oil spray
- UK: 1 small pizza dough ball (store-bought or homemade), 4 tablespoons marinara sauce, 50g mozzarella cheese (shredded), 50g pepperoni slices, 1/4 teaspoon dried oregano, 1/4 teaspoon dried basil, olive oil spray

Instructions:

1. Preheat your air fryer oven to 200°C (390°F).
2. Roll out pizza dough into a circle that fits your air fryer basket.
3. Place dough in the air fryer basket.
4. Spread marinara sauce evenly over the dough, leaving a small border around the edges.
5. Sprinkle mozzarella cheese over the sauce.
6. Arrange pepperoni slices on top of the cheese.
7. Sprinkle dried oregano and basil over the pizza.
8. Lightly spray olive oil over the top of the pizza.
9. Cook for 8-10 minutes until the crust is golden brown and cheese is melted.
10. Remove from air fryer and let cool slightly before slicing and serving.

Nutritional Information:

- Calories: 400 | Fat: 18g | Carbs: 40g | Protein: 16g

Prep: 15 mins | Cook: 25 mins | Serves: 6 servings

Ingredients:

- US: 400g mixed fresh or frozen fruit (e.g., apples, berries, peaches), 50g granulated sugar, 1 tablespoon lemon juice, 75g all-purpose flour, 50g rolled oats, 50g unsalted butter (cold, diced), 50g brown sugar, 1/2 teaspoon ground cinnamon
- UK: 400g mixed fresh or frozen fruit (e.g., apples, berries, peaches), 50g caster sugar, 1 tablespoon lemon juice, 75g plain flour, 50g rolled oats, 50g unsalted butter (cold, diced), 50g soft light brown sugar, 1/2 teaspoon ground cinnamon

Instructions:

1. Preheat your air fryer oven to 180°C (350°F).
2. In a bowl, toss mixed fruit with granulated sugar and lemon juice.
3. Divide fruit mixture among individual ramekins or place in a single baking dish that fits in your air fryer oven.
4. In a separate bowl, combine flour, rolled oats, brown sugar, and cinnamon.
5. Rub cold diced butter into the flour mixture until it resembles coarse crumbs.
6. Sprinkle crumble mixture evenly over the fruit in the ramekins or baking dish.
7. Place ramekins or baking dish in the air fryer basket.
8. Cook for 20-25 minutes until the fruit is bubbly and the topping is golden brown.
9. Remove from air fryer and let cool slightly before serving.
10. Serve warm with a scoop of vanilla ice cream, if desired.

Nutritional Information:

- Calories: 250 | Fat: 10g | Carbs: 40g | Protein: 3g

CHOCOLATE LAVA CAKE

Prep: 15 mins | Cook: 10 mins | Serves: 4 cakes

Ingredients:

- US: 100g dark chocolate (chopped), 75g unsalted butter, 50g granulated sugar, 2 large eggs, 1 teaspoon vanilla extract, 30g all-purpose flour, 1/4 teaspoon salt, oil spray (for greasing)
- UK: 100g dark chocolate (chopped), 75g unsalted butter, 50g caster sugar, 2 large eggs, 1 teaspoon vanilla extract, 30g plain flour, 1/4 teaspoon salt, oil spray (for greasing)

Instructions:

1. Preheat your air fryer oven to 180°C (350°F).
2. Grease 4 ramekins with oil spray.
3. In a microwave-safe bowl, melt chocolate and butter together in short bursts, stirring until smooth.
4. Stir in sugar until combined.
5. Add eggs and vanilla extract, mixing until smooth.
6. Fold in flour and salt until just combined.
7. Divide batter evenly among prepared ramekins.
8. Place ramekins in the air fryer basket.
9. Cook for 8-10 minutes until the edges are set but the centers are still soft.
10. Remove from air fryer and let cool for 1-2 minutes.
11. Carefully invert cakes onto serving plates.
12. Serve immediately, garnished with powdered sugar or a scoop of vanilla ice cream.

Nutritional Information:

- Calories: 350 | Fat: 20g | Carbs: 32g | Protein: 5g

BAKED APPLES

Prep: 10 mins | Cook: 20 mins | Serves: 4 apples

Ingredients:

- US: 4 large apples (such as Granny Smith or Honeycrisp), 50g brown sugar, 1 teaspoon ground cinnamon, 25g unsalted butter (cold, diced), 50g rolled oats, 25g chopped nuts (optional), 50ml apple juice or water
- UK: 4 large apples (such as Granny Smith or Honeycrisp), 50g soft light brown sugar, 1 teaspoon ground cinnamon, 25g unsalted butter (cold, diced), 50g rolled oats, 25g chopped nuts (optional), 50ml apple juice or water

Instructions:

1. Core each apple to create a well for the filling, leaving the bottom intact.
2. In a bowl, combine brown sugar, cinnamon, diced butter, rolled oats, and chopped nuts.
3. Stuff each apple with the oat mixture, pressing down gently.
4. Place stuffed apples in the air fryer basket.
5. Pour apple juice or water into the bottom of the air fryer basket.
6. Cook at 180°C (350°F) for 18-20 minutes until apples are tender and filling is golden brown.
7. Remove from air fryer and let cool slightly before serving.
8. Serve warm, optionally topped with a dollop of whipped cream or vanilla yogurt.

Nutritional Information:

- Calories: 220 | Fat: 8g | Carbs: 38g | Protein: 3g

HOMEMADE CHICKEN NUGGETS

Prep: 15 mins | Cook: 15 mins | Serves: 4

Ingredients:

- US: 500g chicken breast (cut into nugget-sized pieces), 100g breadcrumbs, 50g grated Parmesan cheese, 1 teaspoon garlic powder, 1 teaspoon paprika, salt, pepper, cooking spray
- UK: 500g chicken breast (cut into nugget-sized pieces), 100g breadcrumbs, 50g grated Parmesan cheese, 1 teaspoon garlic powder, 1 teaspoon paprika, salt, pepper, cooking spray

Instructions:

1. Preheat your air fryer oven to 200°C (400°F).
2. Prepare three bowls: one with breadcrumbs, Parmesan, garlic powder, paprika, salt, and pepper each; another with beaten eggs; and the last with flour.
3. Coat each chicken piece in flour, then dip into the egg, and finally coat with the breadcrumb mixture.
4. Arrange nuggets in a single layer in the air fryer basket, ensuring they don't touch.
5. Cook for 10-12 minutes, flipping halfway through, until golden and crispy.
6. Serve hot with your favorite dipping sauce.

Nutritional Information:

- Calories: 300 | Fat: 10g | Carbs: 20g | Protein: 30g

CRISPY TOFU "FISH" AND CHIPS

Prep: 30 mins | Cook: 20 mins | Serves: 4

Ingredients:

- US: 400g firm tofu (cut into "fish" fillets), 100g breadcrumbs, 1 tablespoon Old Bay seasoning, 1 lemon (zested), 4 large potatoes (cut into wedges), salt, pepper, cooking spray, malt vinegar (for serving)
- UK: 400g firm tofu (cut into "fish" fillets), 100g breadcrumbs, 1 tablespoon Old Bay seasoning, 1 lemon (zested), 4 large potatoes (cut into wedges), salt, pepper, cooking spray, malt vinegar (for serving)

Instructions:

1. Preheat your air fryer oven to 200°C (400°F).
2. In a bowl, combine breadcrumbs, Old Bay seasoning, and lemon zest.
3. Coat each tofu fillet in the breadcrumb mixture.
4. Toss potato wedges with salt, pepper, and a light coating of cooking spray.
5. Arrange tofu and potato wedges in the air fryer basket in a single layer.
6. Cook for 15-18 minutes, flipping tofu halfway through, until tofu is crispy and potatoes are tender.
7. Serve hot with malt vinegar.

Nutritional Information:

- Calories: 320 | Fat: 5g | Carbs: 50g | Protein: 15g

CRISPY SPRING ROLLS

Prep: 20 mins | Cook: 15 mins | Serves: 4

Ingredients:

- US: 8 spring roll wrappers, 200g cooked vermicelli noodles, 1 carrot (julienned), 1/2 cabbage (shredded), 100g shrimp (chopped), 2 tablespoons soy sauce, 1 teaspoon sesame oil, salt, pepper, cooking spray
- UK: 8 spring roll wrappers, 200g cooked vermicelli noodles, 1 carrot (julienned), 1/2 cabbage (shredded), 100g shrimp (chopped), 2 tablespoons soy sauce, 1 teaspoon sesame oil, salt, pepper, cooking spray

Instructions:

1. Preheat your air fryer oven to 180°C (350°F).
2. Combine vermicelli noodles, carrot, cabbage, shrimp, soy sauce, sesame oil, salt, and pepper in a bowl.
3. Place a spoonful of filling on each spring roll wrapper, then fold and seal according to package instructions.
4. Lightly spray the rolls with cooking spray.
5. Arrange in the air fryer basket in a single layer.
6. Cook for 12-15 minutes, until golden and crispy.
7. Serve hot with sweet chili sauce.

Nutritional Information:

- Calories: 250 | Fat: 5g | Carbs: 40g | Protein: 10g

SWEET AND SOUR CHICKEN

Prep: 20 mins | Cook: 20 mins | Serves: 4

Ingredients:

- US: 500g chicken breast (cut into bite-sized pieces), 1 bell pepper (diced), 1 onion (diced), 1 can pineapple chunks (drained), 4 tablespoons ketchup, 2 tablespoons soy sauce, 2 tablespoons vinegar, 2 tablespoons brown sugar, salt, pepper, cooking spray
- UK: 500g chicken breast (cut into bite-sized pieces), 1 bell pepper (diced), 1 onion (diced), 1 can pineapple chunks (drained), 4 tablespoons ketchup, 2 tablespoons soy sauce, 2 tablespoons vinegar, 2 tablespoons brown sugar, salt, pepper, cooking spray

Instructions:

1. Preheat your air fryer oven to 200°C (400°F).
2. In a bowl, combine ketchup, soy sauce, vinegar, brown sugar, salt, and pepper to make the sauce.
3. Toss chicken pieces with half of the sauce.
4. Arrange chicken, bell pepper, onion, and pineapple in the air fryer basket.
5. Cook for 15-18 minutes, shaking the basket halfway through, until chicken is cooked through.
6. Drizzle with remaining sauce before serving.

Nutritional Information:

- Calories: 280 | Fat: 5g | Carbs: 35g | Protein: 25g

FALAFEL WRAPS

Prep: 20 mins | Cook: 15 mins | Serves: 4

Ingredients:

- US: 1 can chickpeas (drained and rinsed), 1 small onion (chopped), 2 cloves garlic (minced), 2 tablespoons chopped fresh parsley, 1 teaspoon ground cumin, 1 teaspoon ground coriander, 1/2 teaspoon baking powder, salt, pepper, cooking spray, 4 whole wheat wraps, lettuce, tomato, cucumber (for serving)
- UK: 1 can chickpeas (drained and rinsed), 1 small onion (chopped), 2 cloves garlic (minced), 2 tablespoons chopped fresh parsley, 1 teaspoon ground cumin, 1 teaspoon ground coriander, 1/2 teaspoon baking powder, salt, pepper, cooking spray, 4 whole wheat wraps, lettuce, tomato, cucumber (for serving)

Instructions:

1. Preheat your air fryer oven to 180°C (350°F).
2. In a food processor, blend chickpeas, onion, garlic, parsley, cumin, coriander, baking powder, salt, and pepper until smooth.
3. Form mixture into golf ball-sized balls and flatten slightly.
4. Lightly spray falafel with cooking spray.
5. Arrange in the air fryer basket in a single layer.
6. Cook for 12-15 minutes, flipping halfway through, until golden and crispy.
7. Serve wrapped in whole wheat wraps with lettuce, tomato, and cucumber.

Nutritional Information:

- Calories: 300 | Fat: 8g | Carbs: 45g | Protein: 12g

CHICKEN TIKKA KEBABS

Prep: 25 mins | Cook: 15 mins | Serves: 4

Ingredients:

- US: 500g chicken breast (cut into cubes), 200g plain yogurt, 2 tablespoons tikka masala paste, 1 lemon (juiced), 1 teaspoon ground cumin, 1 teaspoon ground coriander, salt, pepper, cooking spray
- UK: 500g chicken breast (cut into cubes), 200g plain yogurt, 2 tablespoons tikka masala paste, 1 lemon (juiced), 1 teaspoon ground cumin, 1 teaspoon ground coriander, salt, pepper, cooking spray

Instructions:

1. Preheat your air fryer oven to 180°C (350°F).
2. In a bowl, combine yogurt, tikka masala paste, lemon juice, cumin, coriander, salt, and pepper.
3. Add chicken cubes to the marinade, ensuring they are well coated.
4. Thread marinated chicken onto skewers.
5. Lightly spray with cooking spray.
6. Arrange skewers in the air fryer basket in a single layer.
7. Cook for 12-15 minutes, turning skewers halfway through, until chicken is cooked through.
8. Serve hot with naan bread and cucumber yogurt dip.

Nutritional Information:

- Calories: 280 | Fat: 5g | Carbs: 10g | Protein: 35g

CRISPY FISH TACOS

Prep: 20 mins | Cook: 15 mins | Serves: 4

Ingredients:

- US: 500g white fish fillets (cut into strips), 100g breadcrumbs, 1 teaspoon chili powder, 1 teaspoon paprika, 1/2 teaspoon garlic powder, salt, pepper, cooking spray, 8 small corn tortillas, cabbage slaw, lime wedges (for serving)
- UK: 500g white fish fillets (cut into strips), 100g breadcrumbs, 1 teaspoon chili powder, 1 teaspoon paprika, 1/2 teaspoon garlic powder, salt, pepper, cooking spray, 8 small corn tortillas, cabbage slaw, lime wedges (for serving)

Instructions:

1. Preheat your air fryer oven to 200°C (400°F).
2. In a bowl, combine breadcrumbs, chili powder, paprika, garlic powder, salt, and pepper.
3. Coat each fish strip in the breadcrumb mixture.
4. Lightly spray with cooking spray.
5. Arrange fish in the air fryer basket in a single layer.
6. Cook for 10-12 minutes, flipping halfway through, until fish is cooked through and crispy.
7. Serve in corn tortillas with cabbage slaw and lime wedges.

Nutritional Information:

- Calories: 280 | Fat: 5g | Carbs: 30g | Protein: 25g

CRISPY DUCK PANCAKES

Prep: 30 mins | Cook: 20 mins | Serves: 4

Ingredients:

- US: 4 duck breasts (cooked and shredded), 8 Chinese pancakes, 1 cucumber (cut into matchsticks), 4 spring onions (sliced), hoisin sauce, cooking spray
- UK: 4 duck breasts (cooked and shredded), 8 Chinese pancakes, 1 cucumber (cut into matchsticks), 4 spring onions (sliced), hoisin sauce, cooking spray

Instructions:

1. Preheat your air fryer oven to 180°C (350°F).
2. Lightly spray both sides of Chinese pancakes with cooking spray.
3. Arrange pancakes in the air fryer basket in a single layer.
4. Cook for 5-7 minutes, flipping halfway through, until crispy and heated through.
5. Assemble each pancake with shredded duck, cucumber, spring onions, and a drizzle of hoisin sauce.
6. Serve immediately.

Nutritional Information:

- Calories: 350 | Fat: 12g | Carbs: 30g | Protein: 25g

VEGGIE SAMOSAS

Prep: 30 mins | Cook: 15 mins | Serves: 4

Ingredients:

- US: 8 samosa pastry sheets, 2 potatoes (boiled and mashed), 1 cup green peas (cooked), 1 small onion (chopped), 2 cloves garlic (minced), 1 teaspoon curry powder, 1 teaspoon garam masala, salt, pepper, cooking spray
- UK: 8 samosa pastry sheets, 2 potatoes (boiled and mashed), 1 cup green peas (cooked), 1 small onion (chopped), 2 cloves garlic (minced), 1 teaspoon curry powder, 1 teaspoon garam masala, salt, pepper, cooking spray

Instructions:

1. Preheat your air fryer oven to 180°C (350°F).
2. In a bowl, combine mashed potatoes, green peas, onion, garlic, curry powder, garam masala, salt, and pepper.
3. Cut each samosa pastry sheet in half to form rectangles.
4. Place a spoonful of filling on one half of each rectangle, then fold over and seal edges with water.
5. Lightly spray samosas with cooking spray.
6. Arrange in the air fryer basket in a single layer.
7. Cook for 12-15 minutes, until golden and crispy.
8. Serve hot with chutney or yogurt dip.

Nutritional Information:

- Calories: 240 | Fat: 3g | Carbs: 40g | Protein: 8g

VEGETABLE TEMPURA

Prep: 20 mins | Cook: 15 mins | Serves: 4

Ingredients:

- US: Assorted vegetables (such as bell peppers, zucchini, broccoli florets), 100g plain flour, 100ml ice-cold water, 1 egg yolk, salt, pepper, cooking spray
- UK: Assorted vegetables (such as bell peppers, zucchini, broccoli florets), 100g plain flour, 100ml ice-cold water, 1 egg yolk, salt, pepper, cooking spray

Instructions:

1. Preheat your air fryer oven to 200°C (400°F).
2. In a bowl, whisk together flour, ice-cold water, egg yolk, salt, and pepper until smooth.
3. Dip vegetables into the batter, shaking off excess.
4. Lightly spray battered vegetables with cooking spray.
5. Arrange in the air fryer basket in a single layer.
6. Cook for 10-12 minutes, until golden and crispy.
7. Serve hot with soy sauce or tempura dipping sauce.

Nutritional Information:

- Calories: 200 | Fat: 3g | Carbs: 35g | Protein: 5g

ADDITIONAL RESOURCES

CONVERSION CHARTS

Temperature (Celsius to Fahrenheit)

Understanding temperature conversions is crucial when adapting recipes from different sources. Here's a quick reference chart:

Celsius (°C)	Fahrenheit (°F)
150°C	300°F
160°C	320°F
170°C	340°F
180°C	350°F
190°C	375°F
200°C	400°F
210°C	410°F
220°C	425°F

Conversion Formula: $°F = (°C × 9/5) + 32$

Weight and Volume Measurements

For accurate cooking, especially in baking, understanding measurement conversions is essential:
Weight:
- 1 ounce (oz) = 28 grams (g)
- 1 pound (lb) = 454 grams (g)
- 1 kilogram (kg) = 2.2 pounds (lb)

Volume:
- 1 teaspoon (tsp) = 5 millilitres (ml)
- 1 tablespoon (tbsp) = 15 millilitres (ml)
- 1 cup = 240 millilitres (ml)
- 1 pint = 570 millilitres (ml)
- 1 quart = 0.95 litres (L)
- 1 gallon = 3.8 litres (L)

Nutritional Information

Providing a basic nutritional guide for each recipe can be very helpful for readers who are health-conscious or have specific dietary needs. For each recipe, consider including:
- Calories per serving
- Protein (g)
- Carbohydrates (g)
- Fat (g)
- Fibre (g)
- Sodium (mg)

You might also want to include additional information like:
- Serving size
- Preparation time
- Cooking time
- Difficulty level (e.g., Easy, Moderate, Advanced)

Remember to note that nutritional information is an estimate and can vary based on specific ingredients used.

TROUBLESHOOTING GUIDE

A troubleshooting guide can be invaluable for beginners. Here are some common issues and solutions to include:

1. Food Not Crispy Enough:
   - Solution: Spray with a little oil, increase temperature, or cook for longer
2. Food Burning or Cooking Unevenly:
   - Solution: Shake the basket more frequently, reduce temperature, or cut food into more uniform sizes
3. White Smoke Coming from Air Fryer:
   - Solution: This is often due to excess grease. Clean the air fryer thoroughly and reduce the amount of oil used
4. Air Fryer Not Turning On:
   - Solution: Check if it's properly plugged in and the basket is fully inserted
5. Food Sticking to the Basket:
   - Solution: Lightly grease the basket or use parchment paper liners
6. Strange Smell During First Use:
   - Solution: This is normal. Run the air fryer empty at 200°C for about 15 minutes to burn off any manufacturing residues
7. Baked Goods Not Rising Properly:
   - Solution: Don't overfill the basket, which can restrict air flow. Consider using a baking pan designed for air fryers
8. Breading Falling Off:
   - Solution: Ensure food is patted dry before breading, and spray with oil to help breading adhere

GLOSSARY OF COOKING TERMS

A glossary can help beginners understand common cooking terms used throughout the cookbook. Here are some terms to consider including:

1. Air Fry: Cooking food using hot air circulation to achieve a crispy exterior
2. Preheat: Heating the air fryer to the desired temperature before adding food
3. Batch Cooking: Preparing large quantities of food at once for future meals
4. Shake: To move or agitate the air fryer basket to redistribute food for even cooking
5. Flip: To turn food over halfway through cooking for even browning
6. Spray: To lightly coat food with oil using a mister or spray bottle
7. Breadcrumb: Fine particles of dried bread used for coating foods
8. Marinade: A liquid mixture for soaking foods to add flavour before cooking
9. Reheat: To warm up previously cooked food
10. Roast: To cook food in the air fryer, usually at a higher temperature, to achieve a browned exterior
11. Bake: To cook food in the air fryer using lower temperatures, typically for breads and desserts
12. Dehydrate: To remove moisture from foods, often used for making dried fruits or vegetables
13. Non-stick: A coating on the air fryer basket that prevents food from sticking
14. Convection: The circulation of hot air used in air fryers to cook food
15. Maillard Reaction: The browning process that gives food a distinctive flavour and colour

THESE ADDITIONAL RESOURCES WILL MAKE YOUR COOKBOOK MORE COMPREHENSIVE AND USER-FRIENDLY, ESPECIALLY FOR THOSE NEW TO AIR FRYING. THEY PROVIDE VALUABLE REFERENCE INFORMATION THAT READERS CAN EASILY CONSULT AS THEY EXPLORE THE WORLD OF AIR FRYER COOKING.

CONCLUSION

As we come to the end of this culinary journey through the world of air fryer cooking, it's clear that this innovative kitchen appliance has revolutionized the way we prepare and enjoy our favorite foods. From crispy appetizers to succulent main courses and even delectable desserts, the air fryer has proven itself to be a versatile and indispensable tool in the modern kitchen.

Throughout this cookbook, we've explored a wide array of recipes that showcase the air fryer's ability to create delicious, healthier versions of classic dishes. We've discovered how to achieve that perfect golden-brown crispiness without the need for excessive oil, making it possible to indulge in our favorite fried foods with less guilt. The air fryer has shown us that we don't have to sacrifice flavor for health – we can have the best of both worlds.

We've also seen how the air fryer can save us time and energy in the kitchen. With its rapid cooking times and energy-efficient design, it's become a go-to appliance for busy households looking to prepare quick and tasty meals without compromising on quality. The convenience of being able to cook entire meals in one appliance cannot be overstated, especially for those with limited kitchen space or time constraints.

One of the most exciting aspects of air fryer cooking is its ability to inspire creativity in the kitchen. As you've worked your way through these recipes, you may have found yourself thinking of new combinations, flavors, and techniques to try. This cookbook is just the beginning – the possibilities for air fryer cooking are truly endless. We encourage you to continue experimenting, adapting your favorite recipes, and discovering new ways to use your air fryer.

Remember, like any new skill, mastering air fryer cooking takes practice. Don't be discouraged if your first attempts don't turn out exactly as expected. Each recipe you try will teach you something new about your appliance and how different foods respond to air frying. With time and experience, you'll develop an intuitive understanding of how to adjust times and temperatures to achieve the perfect results for your taste preferences.

As you continue your air fryer cooking journey, keep in mind the tips and techniques we've shared throughout this book. Proper maintenance and cleaning of your air fryer will ensure its longevity and consistent performance. Experimenting with different accessories can open up even more cooking possibilities. And don't forget the importance of meal planning and prep – your air fryer can be a valuable ally in creating efficient, delicious meal plans for you and your family.

We hope this cookbook has not only provided you with a collection of delicious recipes but has also inspired you to think differently about cooking. The air fryer represents a shift towards healthier, more convenient cooking methods without sacrificing the flavors and textures we love. It's a testament to how technology can positively impact our daily lives and our relationship with food.

As you close this book and fire up your air fryer, remember that you're part of a growing community of home cooks who are embracing this innovative way of cooking. Share your successes, learn from your challenges, and don't be afraid to put your own spin on these recipes. Cooking is an art as much as it is a science, and your air fryer is a powerful tool in your culinary arsenal.

THANK YOU FOR JOINING US ON THIS FLAVORFUL ADVENTURE. HERE'S TO MANY MORE DELICIOUS, CRISPY, AND HEALTHIER MEALS AHEAD. HAPPY AIR FRYING!

Printed in Great Britain
by Amazon

57317880R00051